Home Life in Bible Times

A STUDY IN BIBLICAL ANTIQUITIES

By ARTHUR W. KLINCK, PH. D.

President, Concordia Teachers College, River Forest, Illinois

Concordia Teacher Training Series

Illustrated by the Author

St. Louis, Mo.
CONCORDIA PUBLISHING HOUSE

FOREWORD

The text *Home Life in Bible Times,* A Study in Biblical Antiquities, aims to make our Sunday school teachers more familiar with the everyday life of Bible people as a background for their understanding and appreciation of the Holy Scriptures and for the improvement of their teaching of Biblical truth.

The Table of Contents shows that no attempt has been made to cover the whole field of Biblical antiquities, which is too large and diversified to be treated in one course of our Concordia series. Thus public life, civil, legal, and military, in New Testament times, the theocratic Old Testament state, the Levitical ordinances, the daily worship, the periodic festivals centering in the Tabernacle and the Temple, and the development of public education in the local synagog, significant and interesting as they are, have been passed over except for a few instances, such as the brief section on religious education in the home. These and other topics will have to wait for treatment in a later course.

No apology is made for the amount of space given to the various topics treated in the text. The author's selection was largely dictated by what he considered to be the needs and interests of Sunday school teachers as he has come to know them through his contacts with many hundreds of them in a variety of areas during the past two decades. Some important material is passed over very briefly because it has been treated so often and so fully elsewhere as to have become common knowledge. Some material has been expanded because of its special value in the personal life and teaching of the religious worker. All of it provides but a series of glimpses into the riches of God's Word in the setting of its human background. If those who read these pages privately or study them in organized classes are led just a little deeper into the beauty and instruction and comfort of the Inspired Writings, the author will feel richly rewarded.

Although the curators of several museums generously

granted permission to reproduce photographs taken in the Near East or in their own archaeological collections, it seemed best for our present purpose not to use half tones, or even to make direct copies, but to present very simple pen-and-ink sketches, giving only essential detail so that Sunday school teachers can readily understand them and even draw some of them on the blackboard in clarification of the Bible History lesson. Many of the author's illustrations are of composite origin, resulting from the comparison of actual ancient remains in the museum collections with their modern Near Eastern equivalent or with a traveler's word picture of it.

In presenting this study the author wishes to express his deep appreciation to all those who during the past ten or eleven years have given him permission to study their collections or have been helpful to him in tracking down one or another small but elusive bit of information. Special gratitude is due Dr. Watson Boyes, Curator of the Oriental Institute Museum, University of Chicago; Prof. C. T. Curelly, Director of the Royal Ontario Museum of Archaeology, Toronto; Dr. H. E. Winlock, Director, and Dr. Ludlow Bull of the Metropolitan Museum of Art, New York; Mrs. Loring Dam, Curator of the Education Department, University of Pennsylvania Museum, Philadelphia; Dr. Sidney Smith, Keeper of the Department of Egytian and Assyrian Antiquities, British Museum, London, for permission to make a detailed study and comparison of the archaeological material under their care, along with pertinent photographs, periodicals, and books in their collections.

To his many colleagues in the ministry and the Christian teaching profession who have been his students in institutes or in formal classes in Biblical Antiquities the author expresses his appreciation for the stimulation and encouragement which made the text seem worth while to begin and follow through. And, finally, to his fellow members on the Sunday School Teacher Training Committee, as well as to the publisher, Mr. O. A. Dorn, he offers sincere thanks for their unfailing co-operation.   A. K.

CONTENTS

[V]

CHAPTER I

Primitive Outdoor Occupations

INTRODUCTION

Man's Work Before and After the Fall. — When God placed man into the Garden of Eden, one of His purposes was that man live a life of wholesome activity. Though the Garden of Eden must have had many beautiful spots suitable for a life of ease and rest, God put man into this garden to *work*, "to dress it and to keep it" (Gen. 2:15). The everyday tasks of the farmer were to be his lot. In sowing and cultivating and pruning and gathering fruit he was to find happiness and contentment and to make a living for himself and for his family. He was to know the feeling of physical well-being that comes with bodily exertion. He was to experience the mental satisfaction of planning his work in advance, so that, according to God's command, he would be able to subdue the earth (Gen. 1:28).

If work was necessary for man's well-being before the Fall, it was doubly necessary after sin had entered the world. Now Adam and Eve began that war with nature which man has had to fight ever since. The ground suffered the curse of God for man's sake. Thorns and thistles hampered his efforts. The earth no longer yielded her fruit. In the sweat of his brow man toiled and ate his bread (Gen. 3:17-19).

Some of the Blessings of Work. — Although the necessity of work must often have seemed to Adam a burdensome curse of God, it was really a blessing in disguise. Through much careful planning and more hard labor he was able to force a living from the reluctant soil, and in the fatigue that followed this hard physical exertion he found peaceful rest. In work, too, he found an antidote for the sins of regretful brooding and despair. Work helped him to curb the sinful desires of his flesh, his pride, and the urge he must often have felt to blame Eve for the fallen state of the race. The sons of Adam and Eve learned to work as farmers and shepherds, thus dividing the chief tasks of their father. Cain's work and sacrifice were in themselves no less honorable than Abel's, but they failed to bring him satisfaction and blessing, because his heart was not right (Gen. 4:5 f.). He had evidently lost his faith and trust in God, and, unrepentant and rebellious as he was, he permitted his mind to brood over God's favorable reception of Abel's sacrifices. Abel's whole attitude toward his labor and its blessings was shown by his cheerful willingness to devote the firstlings of his flock to the Lord (Gen. 4:4). And ever since, in the measure in which men have gone about their daily tasks, with faith and gratitude toward God and with intelligent interest and steady industry, they have, with His blessing, not only built sturdy, self-reliant characters, but have escaped many of the temptations which beset those whose heart, because of ingratitude and resentment, is not in their work.

Rugged Palestine as the Home of God's People. — God called Abraham, the ancestor of His chosen people, out of the rich Tigris-Euphrates valley to live in the mountains of Canaan. From the Promised Land He took the patriarchal family to the fertile delta region of northern Egypt. He led their descendants about in the wilderness of Sinai for a generation. But these periods were only seasons of preparation for their role in world history. His people were not to be wealthy landlords or peasant slaves in Egypt or Babylonia, nor were they to become restless, wandering, fighting desert tribes. God chose for their permanent home the land of Canaan, where they could become a freedom-loving, independent people, each with his own farm or his own vineyard.

The Struggle for Existence and Its Results. — In Canaan God's people could make their living as shepherds, but only through ceaseless watchfulness, industry, and faithfulness in their lonely task of caring for their flocks. Here they could wrest a good living from the soil, but only by long and backbreaking hours of labor. Here, too, they could grow grapes and other fruits successfully, but only by terracing the mountain slopes, maintaining the stone-terrace walls, and guarding the vineyards against marauding men and animals. Only by careful planning and generations of devoted work could the country be made and kept "a land of brooks of water, of fountains and depths, that spring out of valleys and hills, a land of wheat and barley and vines and fig trees and pomegranates, a land of oil olive and honey" (Deut. 8:7-8).

In this chosen land the people of Israel were to find and work out their God-given destiny. As a result of their continuous struggle for existence, the hardy mountain shepherds and vinedressers, the farmers of the lowlands, the fishermen of Galilee and of the Mediterranean coast built up a strong and self-reliant people, able to support itself and to defend itself against its enemies. Such was the blood of Samuel and David and Amos and Isaiah, of Jesus and Peter and John and Paul.

The Value of Studying Ancient Customs. — What was the daily life of these people? How did they earn their living? What did they eat and drink and wear? How did they find shelter from heat and cold and rain? What were their interests and social customs? These questions are important, for, though the Bible truths apply to all mankind, the Bible itself is built around the history of a people. Its characters act according to the customs of that people. Its parables are based upon their daily life and activities. As we learn about these people, we shall feel more and more at home with them and grow in our understanding not only of Bible history, but also of the parables and the laws and the sermons and the doctrines which the Holy Spirit has woven into the historical pattern of the Scriptures.

HUNTING

Reasons for Engaging in Hunting. — God expressly gave Noah and his sons the privilege of using animals for food (Gen. 9:3), but the first mention of hunting occurs in the case of Nimrod, "a mighty hunter before the Lord" (Gen. 10:9), who probably, as commentators have suggested, hunted wild animals for sport and adventure in the manner of the Babylonian nobility. David, on the contrary, had to kill a lion and a bear in order to protect his flocks (1 Sam. 17:34-37). Esau went out to the field to hunt wild game

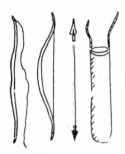

from which to prepare "savory meat," such as his father loved (Gen. 27:4). Thus from the earliest times the Hebrew people hunted wild animals and fowl in order to supplement their scant meat supply. By eating deer, gazelle, antelope, mountain sheep and goats, and other "clean" animals, as well as the various "clean" birds, the Judean farmer could spare his domestic flocks and herds, thus preserving his source of milk and wool.

Bows, arrowhead, arrow, and quiver

Weapons Used in Hunting. — The hunting weapons mentioned in the Bible are those common to most ancient nations.

The bow and arrow appear very early in the history of God's people and throughout Biblical times (Gen. 27:3). The *bow,* made of wood, was small compared with the powerful longbow of the later North European races. It was strung with a thong of gut, hide, or sinew or with a cord made of waxed cotton or linen. The *arrows* were of approximately lead-pencil thickness. Made of straight reeds or cut from straight-grained wood, they were tipped with bronze or iron arrowheads. The *quiver,* resembling a small golf bag, slung over the shoulder of the hunter, had a capacity of a dozen or more arrows.

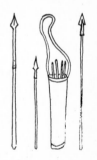

The short spears, or *darts,* for close hunting, the longer spear, or *javelin,* for long-distance throwing, as well as the *lance,* used like a modern bayonet for thrusting, were shafts of wood varying in length from three to seven feet, ending in bronze or iron spearheads.

Lance, dart, quiver, and javelin

The young Israelite became adept in the use of the *sling*, which might be his own six-foot sash of cloth. Holding one end of the sash firmly by winding it around his fingers and gripping the other end between his thumb and forefinger, the slinger placed a stone into the loop of the cloth. He then swung it rapidly at arm's length until, when it had attained great momentum, he released the loosely held end, permitting the stone to fly to its target. Used with an egg-sized stone as a missile, the sling was a powerful weapon,

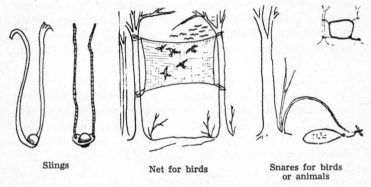

Slings   Net for birds   Snares for birds
or animals

capable of killing the hardiest of wild animals. We need not be surprised that the stone slung by David sank deep into the forehead of Goliath, killing him instantly (1 Sam. 17:49-50).

Methods Used in Trapping Animals and Birds. — In order to catch the smaller animals or birds, the hunter used various types of *nets* and *snares*. He might stretch a coarse-meshed net among the branches of trees along the route followed by birds in flight. He might make a noose of strong cord, one end of which he tied to the end of a sapling which he had bent over and pegged to the ground. When a bird or animal pulled or scratched at the bait, the sapling snapped free from the peg and jerked the noose upwards, suspending the victim in mid-air (Jer. 5:26; Prov. 7:23; Ps. 124:7; Amos 3:5). Larger clean animals, such as gazelles or goats, as well as marauding lions, jackals, and other beasts of prey, were

commonly caught in *pits*. Dug into the path usually followed by the animals as they went to drink, the pit was
covered with a loose framework of small tree branches and
reeds over which a thin layer of earth was carefully packed.
This seemingly innocent part of the path gave way suddenly at the slightest pressure, throwing the unsuspecting
animal into the pit, where it was at the mercy of the hunter
(2 Sam. 23:20).

Humane Treatment of Animals. — In order that the supply of wild life might not be exhausted, the Hebrew law
declared a closed season on game animals and birds every
seventh year and allowed them to eat the balance of the
unharvested crop after the poor had had their fill (Ex. 23:
11; Lev. 25:7).

In appreciation of God's mercy to man, God expected
him to be merciful to animals, a lesson which Christian
teachers can well afford to impress upon their children (Ps.
104:21; Ps. 147:9; Job 38:41). The blood of animals killed
for food was permitted to soak into the ground, or it was
reverently covered with dust (Lev. 17:13).

FISHING

Israelite Knowledge of Fishing. — The Old Testament
does not describe the process of fishing; yet from quite a
number of allusions to that occupation we know that the
Israelites knew about it, and they doubtless also practiced
it to supplement their meat supply (Ezek. 47:10). In the
wilderness the wandering tribes complained to Moses that
he had deprived them of the fish of Egypt (Num. 11:5).
At the time of Nehemiah, fish were sold on the market in
Jerusalem (Neh. 13:16), and one entrance to Jerusalem had
already been named the "Fish Gate," no doubt because of
the fish market in its vicinity (Neh. 12:39; 2 Chron. 33:14).
While the Old Testament contains only passing references,
the New Testament gives us several extended accounts of
fishing. Some of Jesus' disciples had made their living by
fishing on Lake Galilee before they began to follow Jesus,

and occasionally they went back to their former occupation for a short time (Matt. 4:21; Luke 5:5 f.; John 21:3 f.).

The Use of the Net. — Galilean fishermen used *nets* of various types, with mesh varying from coarse to fine according to the kind of fish they intended to catch. The *dip net* consisted of a cone-shaped mesh held open by a wooden hoop formed from the thin end of a newly cut branch, the thicker end of which served as a handle. The *casting net* was thrown out into the water and then, by means of ropes, pulled back openmouthed to the shore. The *dragnet,* about as long as a tennis net and perhaps three times as high, was

Casting net and dip net

Dragnet between boats

stretched between two boats. Its top kept at the water level by a series of floats and the opposite edge held down by sinkers, the submerged net was dragged toward the shore between the boats, enclosing whatever fish happened to be in its way. In one of His parables Jesus compares the kingdom of heaven to this type of net. Just as the dragnet brings all kinds of fish to the shore, where the fishermen separate the good from the bad, "so shall it be at the end of the world; the angels shall come forth and sever the wicked from among the just" (Matt. 13:47-50). Fishing on Lake Galilee was carried on largely by night, when the fish came in close to the shore to feed (Luke 5:5; John 21:3-6).

Fishing with Hooks. — Fishhooks are mentioned in Amos 4:2; Ezek. 29:4; and in Matt. 17:27. No doubt they were used as extensively by Israel as by other neighboring peoples.

All sizes of ancient hooks of iron and bronze have been preserved, from light ones, not over an inch in length, to very strong ones, capable of catching and holding the largest fish of the Nile. The shape of the ancient fishhooks is very much like those of our own day. The "hooks" mentioned in Amos 4:2 may refer to grappling hooks by means of which fish were pulled from the nets into the boats.

The Fish Spear, or Harpoon. — The Egyptian fisherman permitted his boat to drift down the Nile while, statuelike, he knelt at the edge of the deck with spear poised, ready to drive it into the body of any large fish he might see. Though

Ancient fishhooks

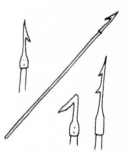

Harpoon, or fish spear, and grappling hook

during their sojourn in Egypt the Israelites certainly learned this use of spears or harpoons in the rich waters of the Egyptian delta, there is no Biblical reference to this type of fishing in the Lake of Galilee or in the Jordan River.

"Fishers of Men." — As fishermen, men like Peter and James and John had learned the value of hard work. They had learned to endure the disappointment of fishing a whole night and catching nothing. They had practiced patience through many a long hour of waiting. They had dared to face the treacherous storms of Lake Galilee. It was not by accident that Jesus chose people of this occupation to become "fishers of men," an occupation in which they could use all the patience and strength and perseverance and courage which they had learned (Matt. 4:19).

GRAZING AND SHEEP RAISING

Ranching in the East Country. — Much of the wind-swept plateau east of the Jordan River was cattle country like our Southwest, and the "strong bulls of Bashan" (Ps. 22:12) were as proverbial as our own "Texas longhorns." Pasturing their cattle in the open the year round, the nomadic ranchers lived largely on meat and milk products, supplemented by the wild fruits, nuts, and herbs of the field, rather than by the products of a settled agriculture. They counted their wealth in cattle, the meat and hides of which furnished food and raw materials for export to the larger cities. Great herds of asses, and even of horses, grazed on the grassy uplands and in the valleys, while on the fringes of the Syrian desert, camels were the chief source of wealth. Like Abraham, Job was a great rancher, with vast herds of sheep, camels, oxen, and asses (Job 1:3).

Hog Raising. — Hogs, unclean according to the Mosaic Law (Lev. 11:7), were not raised by the Israelites themselves, but in the "far country," where, according to Luke 15:13-16, the Prodigal Son wasted his substance and finally had to make his living by herding the hogs of a heathen citizen. And in the country of the Gadarenes (Mark 5:11 f.), pigs were kept in large numbers by the non-Jewish population, as indeed they have been by most peoples throughout world history.

The Raising of Sheep and Goats. — In Palestine proper, west of the Jordan, the land on which large herds of cattle could have grazed was too necessary for agricultural purposes to be set aside for pasture. A farmer might have a cow or two, or a yoke of oxen which he used to draw his wagon and agricultural implements. He used donkeys as beasts of burden about his farm and vineyard. He might even keep one camel for the same purpose. But the animals found in very large numbers were the sheep and goats, which could find a living, in the uncleared "wilderness" (Luke 15:4), on the steep slopes and crags and in the ravines of the mountainous regions inaccessible to the larger cattle. Such flocks occupied the attention of a considerable part of the population.

The Equipment of the Shepherd. — The shepherd might be a village dweller who either devoted part of his time to the herding of sheep besides carrying on agriculture or gave all of his energies to the work of caring for his flock. In either case he needed about the same type of equipment. Since he had to be self-sufficient for days or weeks at a time

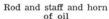

Rod and staff and horn of oil

Shepherd's purse

while he was pasturing his sheep in out-of-the-way places, his kit had to be compact and light enough so that he could carry it along with him.

For the protection of his sheep he needed his *"rod and staff"* (Ps. 23:4). The rod was a club about two feet long, the thinner end of which he gripped in his hand or attached to his sash by a leather cord strung through a hole in the handle. This was a formidable weapon for the defense of his sheep against robbers or wild animals. The shepherd used his staff, a straight sapling about six or seven feet long, to guide his sheep, to knock off twigs and leaves from the trees for their food, and to assist himself in climbing steep and rocky hillsides and treacherous ravines in search of food, water, and shelter for his flock. (The traditional shepherd's crook of Christian art seems to be a European rather than a Palestinian staff.)

Like the hunter, the shepherd carried his sling and a few smooth stones in his shepherd's bag, or purse, for defense against marauders, animal or human (1 Sam. 17:40). His purse also held his noonday lunch of dried figs or raisins, cheese and bread, or parched wheat. At his sash hung a clay flask or a hollow gourd which served as a container for water. He might also carry a horn of olive oil in the same way. His heavy cloak of sheepskin or of homespun wool, draped over his shoulders and held in with a sash at the waist, served him as a coat by day and a cover by night. In the fold above his sash at his bosom he could find room for a sick or injured lamb (Is. 40:11) which would have perished without his help. On his head he wore the usual square of cotton cloth, held in place about his temples by a woven halo of wool. Thus equipped, he was ready to battle the elements or his enemies in the care and defense of his sheep.

The Construction of the Sheepfold. — The sheepfold might be a cave reaching far back into the limestone cliff. Such caves have been occupied in Palestine by successive generations of shepherds since the days of the judges, and

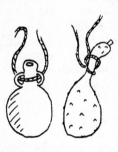

Pottery flask and gourd of water

Cave sheepfold

even of Israel's predecessors, the Canaanite tribes. In front of the cave the shepherd might build a wall of rock, about six feet high, with only one door through which he and his sheep could enter (John 10:1). Thus the sheep would have a warm stable and a courtyard where they could be protected from their enemies and yet sleep in the open air in pleasant weather.

Sheepfold built of rock

Where caves were not available, the shepherd built his enclosing wall of rock in the same way (Num. 32:16), but roofed it over at one end in order to make a weatherproof stable for the sheep. The interior of the stable was reached by archways opening out into the court. Such a sheepfold, surrounded by its stone wall and defended by the shepherds, became a fortress for the protection of the sheep.

THE SHEPHERD AND HIS SHEEP

Pasturing the Sheep. — In the mountains of Judea there were few safe, open meadows where sheep could be left unguarded by day or night. In the daytime the shepherd sought out the best pasture, away back in the recesses of a winding ravine or on a grassy slope which he could reach only by carefully leading the sheep over dangerous mountain paths. He led them to the still waters, where they could drink without danger of falling into the swift current or the terrifying rapids. He let them rest in the shade of the trees or where some great rock cast a welcome shadow (Is. 32:2). While they rested, he watched, meanwhile playing simple music on a shepherd's pipe, which he could lay aside in a second in order to free his hands for the use of his sling or his club.

Back to the Fold. — At the first sign of a threatening storm, or in any case by midafternoon, he called his sheep together and headed for home, so as not to risk their lives either in a sudden flood or in the darkness. The shepherd did not drive his sheep, but walked ahead of them, calling gently to those that showed signs of weariness and carefully seeing that each wanderer returned to the flock. Then, standing in his sheepfold doorway, he called them by name as they crowded past him, again making sure that none was missing. Flocks might be as small as a dozen or two, or they might run up to at least one hundred, as we see from the Parable of the Lost Sheep (Luke 15:4).

Dangers of the Night. — But not all the danger was past when the shepherd had led his sheep safely into the fold. The enemy might strike in the dead of night, so the shepherd watched over his flocks from the top of the wall or roof or dozed by his campfire while the flock slept. In case of an attack by robbers or by wolves a shepherd worthy of the name did not flee, but was ready to give his life for his sheep. With no thought of self-preservation, he bravely stood up against his enemies until either he or they were defeated.

The Good Shepherd. — What a picture the shepherd passages give us of the Savior! No wonder the Lord chose the dependence of sheep upon the shepherd to explain the relationship between Himself and His people. He is the Keeper of Israel, who neither slumbers nor sleeps (Ps. 121: 4; Ps. 80:1). It is He who makes His sheep to lie down in green pastures and leads them beside the still waters (Ps. 23:2), feeding His flock like a shepherd (Is. 40:11). Even in the valley where death casts its terrifying shadows, they need not fear, for He is with them, comforting them with His reassuring presence (Ps. 23:4). "All we like sheep have gone astray; we have turned everyone to his own way," and, instead of punishing us, "The Lord hath laid upon Him the iniquity of us all. He was oppressed and He was afflicted" (Is. 53:6-7). This prophetic passage finds its fulfillment in Jesus, the Good Shepherd, who "giveth His life for the sheep" (John 10:11; John 19:30). He it is who restores those who have strayed away (1 Pet. 2:25), carrying them home upon His shoulders rejoicing (Luke 15:5). It is He who turns them over to undershepherds like Peter, and all Christian pastors and teachers since, with the commission "Feed My lambs . . . feed My sheep," a commission which has as its one great condition the searching question "Lovest thou Me?" (John 21:15-17.) And, with this vital condition fulfilled, in the measure that we become better acquainted with our Good Shepherd and study His Word and imitate His methods and, above all, reflect more and more of His unselfish love, we

shall be successful in finding and bringing in and teaching
His lambs, until there will be "one fold and one Shepherd"
(John 10:16).

REVIEW QUESTIONS AND EXERCISES

1. Enumerate the advantages of a definite work program for man
   a) before the Fall
   b) after the Fall
2. What were some of the advantages of Palestine as compared
   with the Nile Delta or the Sinai Desert as a permanent home
   for God's people?
3. In connection with the occupation of hunting be prepared to
   sketch roughly and to describe briefly the method of using the
   following:
   a) bow and arrow and quiver
   b) darts, javelin, and lance
   c) the sling and its missile
   d) nets and snares
   e) pits
4. Describe and sketch the following equipment of the Palestinian
   fisherman:
   a) dip net
   b) dragnet
   c) casting net
   d) hook
   e) harpoon
5. Picture the environment and life of the people in the cattle
   country east of the Jordan and on the fringes of the Syrian
   Desert.
6. Why was Palestine proper largely devoted to the raising of
   sheep? Describe a sheepfold.
7. Describe the shepherd's equipment:
   a) rod and staff
   b) purse and its contents
   c) horn of oil and its uses
8. Study and be ready to interpret briefly
   a) Psalm 23
   b) The Parable of the Good Shepherd
   c) The Parable of the Lost Sheep

PROBLEMS FOR FURTHER STUDY

1. What motivation can you furnish for Sunday school children to
   look forward to a useful life rather than to a life of ease?
2. How can the mercy and forethought of God in the preservation
   of wild life be used in properly molding the attitudes of children
   toward animals?

3. Through a study of the New Testament passages concerning fishing, develop the thought in Jesus' words "I will make you fishers of men" (Matt. 4:19).
4. Study Psalm 22, and try to determine what the suffering Savior means by "wild bulls of Bashan have beset Me round."
5. Compare the character and actions of
      a) the sheep and the goats
      b) the hireling and the shepherd
and develop an application of each to the life of the class or the teacher or both.

CHAPTER II

Agriculture

The hunter or the shepherd may wander from place to place, pitching his tent wherever he can find pasture and water, as Abraham and the other patriarchs did during their sojourn in Canaan. The farmer, on the contrary, must have a plot of ground which will be his fixed home, with at least some assurance of permanence. He will have little enthusiasm for the hard work of plowing and sowing if he suspects that someone else will harvest his crop. Nor will he develop a real love for his particular plot of ground and try to improve it from year to year if he knows that after his death it will pass out of his family forever. It was God's intention that Israel should become a settled nation as quickly as possible after their wanderings in the Sinai Wilderness.

THE LAND

Palestine's Condition at the Time of Joshua. — The rugged Palestinian country required more than a few years, more than a few generations of devoted farmers, to raise it to its highest productivity. The highly civilized Canaanites had been improving the land for generations during Israel's stay in Egypt and in the wilderness, and had carried on agriculture so well that in addition to the large areas of Palestine which were extremely rich by nature (Ex. 3:8), they had made out of many a steep hillside or barren crest another piece of "land flowing with milk and honey."

After the conquest the Israelites gradually took over this improved land. Joshua assigned to each tribe a province, to each household a certain small section of land which was to be the family inheritance forever (Josh. 13 and 14). Allowing a comparatively thin population for the wildest mountain

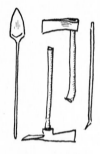

regions of the highland ridge, the most barren sandhills of the south, and the dry grazing lands of the eastern plateau, we can estimate that the average Israelite received from six to ten acres on which to provide a living for his family.

Types of Land: Improvement by Clearing and Terracing. — The small family plot might include widely varying types of soil. Here was a secluded valley which would yield rich crops at once. There an old Canaanite terrace wall had

Shovel, mattock, ax, and crowbar

fallen down and needed immediate attention. Here a steep hillside, strewn with boulders and covered with underbrush, would serve for the time being only as pasture land for the sheep and goats, but it could gradually be made into excellent farm land. The farmer could clear away the bushes and weeds with shovel, ax, and mattock. One by one he could pick up or dig out the boulders. He and his sons,

A terraced hillside

with the help of the oxen, could drag them down the hill a few yards and build them up into a strong retaining wall, roughly following the contour of the hillside. As time permitted, they could fill in behind the wall with earth until they had formed a section of level terrace where next year they could plant a little more wheat or barley or vegetables. As more farm land was needed, more could be provided in the same way until the whole hillside was covered with fertile terraces. Thus in the course of time thousands upon thousands of acres of almost useless land, reclaimed from the erosive force of wind and water, were transformed into a "garden of the Lord" (Is. 51:3). It was backbreaking work, requiring endless patience, perseverance, devotion, faith. But where these qualities were needed, they were supplied. While the Israelites were gradually making new land, the land was making them. It gradually transformed those timid Egyptian slaves, those restless wanderers from the Sinai Desert into proud home owners, passionate home lovers, patriots. Throughout her history as an independent nation, Israel's agricultural products were the mainstay of her national wealth, and the rugged men of the soil, along with her fearless shepherds, were the backbone of her national defense.

The Use of Irrigation in Bible Lands. — To what extent the Israelites employed the processes of irrigation which they had learned in Egypt or those which were in use in other neighboring countries, we do not know, but a few of these ancient

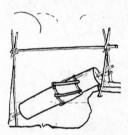

Cylinder irrigation device

irrigation machines will be of interest. Unless a convenient stream or spring provided an abundance of water at a high enough level to flow into the gardens or fields, a device had to be used to raise the water a few feet from a well or cistern or from a spring or river.

One of these irrigation machines consisted of a hollow wooden cylinder with an axle set at an angle of about 30 degrees from the horizontal. Fixed to the inner side of the cylinder was a screw extending from end to end in a continuous spiral, like the grain conveyers used in our elevators. Holding on to a convenient support with his hands, the gardener tramped up steps of wood attached to the cylinder. While he apparently walked up the steps, the cylinder turned instead, and his body remained in the same position. The water, entering the lower end of the cylinder, was forced upwards by the inner spiral until it poured in a steady stream from the upper ends into a trough that carried it where it was needed.

Another device consisted of a continuous row of pottery cups or jars fixed to an endless belt of tarred rope which passed over two grooved wheels. As the operator turned the upper wheel with a crank or, through an arrangement of wooden cogs, by the power of a donkey or camel, cup after cup passed upside down under the surface of water, went around the lower wheel, and came upright on the other side, full of water. As it approached the highest point on

Cup-type irrigation
machine

the upper wheel, it turned over gradually, pouring out its contents into a trough arranged to catch it. Shallow-well pumps working on this same principle are in use in many parts of our country today. The "wheel, broken at the cistern," is a symbol of the termination of man's useful activity through death (Eccl. 12:6).

A third machine used in the rivers of Persia and Syria was a very large water wheel, turned by the force of the stream itself. As the current revolved the wheel, cups of pottery or sacks of cloth, water-proofed with tar, carried the water to the topmost level of the wheel, where, as in the previous case, it spilled into a trough provided for that purpose. In this way the ancient peoples raised large quantities of water to the storage tanks and aqueducts which supplied the people of the city with drinking water and those of the country district with water for irrigation.

PLOWING AND SOWING

Primitive Cultivation by Hand. — The processes of agriculture have always been determined to a very large extent by the power available to the farmer. Where the plot of land was small and manpower only was available, the people laboriously dug up the ground with a crude shovel of wood or of iron. Even the comparatively poor, however, might have the use of at least a donkey or a cow, while yokes of oxen are mentioned throughout Scripture. Oxen appear to have been the usual draft animals, as donkeys and camels were the beasts of burden.

Harnessing Animal Power; the Yoke. — The harness of the oxen was very simple, consisting of a yoke by which the animals were fastened to each other and then hitched to the beam, or the tongue, of the agricultural implement.

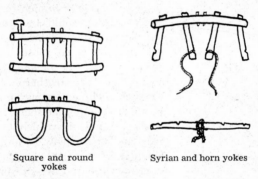

Square and round
yokes

Syrian and horn yokes

The yokes were of wood, constructed in various ways. The *horn yoke* was simply a branch of a tree, perhaps five feet in length and from two to three inches in diameter, which was bound across the horns of two animals as they stood side by side. This type of yoke is particularly common on the Egyptian monuments. The *square yoke* consisted of two horizontal beams fastened together in such a way as to provide two rectangular openings in which the necks of the animals were confined by long pegs inserted vertically into holes at the ends of the beams. *Round yokes* were made by bending green saplings into U-shaped neck pieces and inserting the ends upward into holes in the yoke beam, where they were bound fast or held in place by small horizontal pegs. The modern *Syrian yoke,* no doubt also used in ancient times, has four flat pieces of wood, each about 20 inches long, projecting downward almost perpendicular to the beam. Thongs of hide or rope then complete the encirclement of the animal's neck. Any of these yokes might be bound to the tug rope or to the tongue of the implement. They might also have a hole in the center through which the tongue of the implement was passed and then pegged or bound into place.

The Plow and Goad. — The Palestinian *plow* was a crude and extremely inefficient instrument. In its most primitive form it was probably cut from a naturally forked bough of

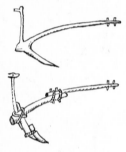

Palestinian plows

a tree. One long branch formed the tongue which could be attached to the yoke. Another branch, extending at a somewhat acute angle from the first, was cut off and sharpened to become the plowshare. Still another branch, extending in the opposite direction to the share, furnished a short handle by which the workman guided his plow. Plows of this kind were common throughout the ancient world and are still in use today in primitive sections of India, China, Africa, and the Near East.

All ancient Palestinian plows seem to have been adaptations of the simple one described above. Because of the scarcity of good timber the draft beam was often made in two pieces, pegged and bound together. Pegs were set into the front end of the draft beam and a broad mortise was cut at an angle near the opposite end to receive the share beam and the handle, which were then tightly bound or clamped into place. The share might be shod with a stone or iron point. Yet such a plow was very little more efficient than the all-wooden instruments described above, since the share was not designed to cut a furrow and turn it over but simply to tear up the ground in an irregular, haphazard way. It is remarkable that the never-changing East has left even the most useful agricultural implement invented by man in this crude and unimproved form for thousands of years.

In order to keep his animals in motion the driver used a *goad,* a long pole shod at one end with a chisel-shaped piece of bronze or iron. Though this chisel end was designed to be used in cleaning the mud off the plowshare, it might also serve to curb stubborn oxen. It is this use to which Jesus refers when He tells badly shaken Saul of Tarsus, "It is hard for thee to kick against the pricks" (R. V., "goad") (Acts 9:5). It was one of these goads, too, that Shamgar used, as an improvised spear, to kill 600 Philistines (Judg. 3:31).

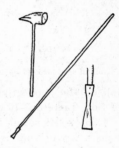

Wooden mattock, ox goad, and chisel point of a goad

Preparing the Plowed Land for Sowing. — After the plow had torn up the ground, the plowman walked along the rough furrows and broke up the lumps with a mattock of wood or of iron (Is. 28:24-25). He might then yoke his oxen to a harrow of brushwood and drive them back and forth to rake the ground fine. If he was particularly progressive, his harrow might consist

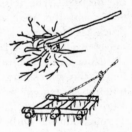

Brushwood harrow and spike-toothed harrow

of a wooden platform in which were set bits of iron or stone, or it might be a framework of heavy beams into which long iron spikes had been driven. The preparation of the soil took place during the fall, beginning in October, immediately after the early rains had softened the hard-baked soil of summer.

Sowing the Seed. — Either immediately before the process of plowing or immediately after the ground had been prepared, "a sower went forth to sow his seed." Carrying the

Ancient seed baskets

grain in a basket or a sack, or even in a fold of his garment held between his left arm and his body, he walked back and forth across the field, sowing the seed broadcast with his right hand. In spite of his painstaking care it happened that some fell by the wayside and was trodden down and the birds of the air devoured it, while some fell in the shallow soil upon the rock or among the thorns. Most of it, of course, fell on the good ground. (The Parable of the Four Kinds of Soil, Luke 8:5-15.)

After the sower followed the ox-drawn harrow or perhaps a boy driving before him all the sheep and goats and calves, whose sharp hoofs trampled the seed into the ground. The job of sowing was done, and the seed was left to the processes of nature. (The seed growing of itself, Mark 4:26-29.)

Now came the rains. Intermittently the sun shone, and the grain quickly sprang up so that the fields were green by mid-November. Throughout the chill months of De-

Egyptian sickle and jawbone sickle

cember and January the grain remained fairly short, beginning to grow noticeably toward the end of March. When the heat and drought of late spring finally came, the seed head matured with surprising rapidity. The grain most commonly grown for human use was wheat, while barley was reserved as food for the animals.*

CUTTING AND BINDING THE GRAIN

Sickles Used in Cutting the Grain. — The Israelite farmer harvested his grain with a sickle. Early sickles seem to have been made of one half of the lower jawbone of an

---

* The word "corn" as used in the Bible means grain. It has no relation to our American corn.

ass or a cow. It appears that, as the teeth became loosened, they were removed and replaced by small chisel-shaped pieces of flint, hammered into the tooth sockets and caulked tightly with pitch or asphalt. The Egyptians made a similarly shaped sickle out of wood, also set with flints secured in a wooden blade. Sickles of glazed pottery have been unearthed in the ruins of ancient Canaanite cities. Parallel with these more primitive instruments, and no doubt gradually crowding them out of common use, were the more efficient and more modern-looking sickles of bronze or iron set in wooden handles. These were of many shapes and sizes, from almost straight knifelike blades to our own familiar

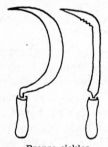 

Bronze sickles   Wooden rake and sheaf of wheat

crescent-shaped type. Some even had saw teeth toward the pointed end of the cutting edge. The Palestinians apparently knew nothing of the large two-handed scythe nor of the wooden-fingered cradle used by our own ancestors until the invention of the mechanical mower and binder.

Gathering and Binding the Grain; the Gleaners. — The reaper cut the grain and laid it on the ground to be raked together and picked up by a man who bound it into sheaves by means of a handful of its own straw. God's law forbade the binder to pick up what had fallen to the ground or had been missed when he gathered his armful of wheat. This he must leave for the poor gleaners, who, like Ruth the Moabitess (Ruth 2:2-3), came out to the harvest field to gather their scant rations for the coming year.

Drying and Transporting the Sheaves to the Threshing Floor. — It was not necessary to set the bundles of grain up into shocks, since rains in the harvest season were so unusual as to be considered miraculous (Jer. 5:24; Song of Sol. 2:11; Joel 2:23; 1 Kings 8:35). From the field the grain was transported to the

Wooden cart with rack

threshing floor on a simple rack fixed to a cart or bound on the back of a donkey. Two men might carry a load of grain on a litterlike frame of light poles, which held quite a good-sized heap.

THRESHING AND WINNOWING

Preparing the Threshing Floor. — On the most convenient bare hilltop a circular plot of ground from 30 to 60 feet in diameter was reserved for threshing purposes from year to year. From the time of the spring rains the ground was kept leveled and rolled until its surface resembled that of a modern clay tennis court. Some threshing floors made use of the natural limestone rock, quarried smooth, with the crevices and depressions filled in with clay. Usually a low wall of stones set bounds to the actual threshing area.

Threshing by Means of Cattle. — Using a wooden pitchfork, the farmer threw the bundles from the wagon to the threshing floor. Other men cut them open and spread them as uniformly as possible over the whole area to a depth of about a foot. Then the actual threshing process began. Cows, calves, sheep, and donkeys, driven around and around the floor, tramped the grain out of the straw and chaff. The animals wore no muzzles, as they do on modern Arabian threshing floors, for the Law of Moses had commanded: "Thou shalt not muzzle the ox

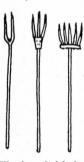

Wooden pitchforks

when he treadeth out the corn" (Deut. 25:4). Sometimes the animals wore blinders over their eyes so that they would not become dizzy from the circular motion.

Threshing Machines Drawn by Oxen. — Along with the cattle a threshing machine might be used. These were of several types. One looked very much like the harrow described above. A wooden platform, about four feet by six or seven feet, bent up slightly in front to enable it to slide easily over the straw, was fitted with bits of stone or sharp teeth of iron on its bottom surface so that it might tear the straw and bruise the grain from the seed heads. Another

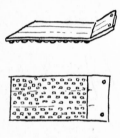

Threshing sled shod
with stones

Threshing sled with
disc wheels

threshing machine consisted of a heavy frame in the shape of a sled mounted on three broad rollers. Each roller was fitted with three or four iron disks, forming eleven disk wheels in all, which cut and ground and crushed the grain as a team of oxen dragged the machine about the threshing floor.

An Egyptian Threshing Device. — The ancient Egyptians used another threshing device, which may also have been introduced into Palestine by the Israelites. It looked very much like a small diving board firmly fixed in the ground at one end and sloping upward towards the free end at an angle of perhaps 20 degrees. From the free end projected several rows of long wooden or metal spikes. The thresher swung a sheaf up over his head, then brought it down sharply so that the head ends of the stalks were forced between the spokes. Then he pulled the sheaf upwards, stripping the ripe wheat out of the ear. The grain and chaff fell to the ground below the board, while the straw was thrown aside. The fundamental principle of this device is still used in the ordinary spiked-cylinder threshing machine of today.

The Use of the Flail. — Sometimes the farmer chose to beat out the grain with a flail, as our own great-grandfathers did. This consisted of a short wooden handle bound by means of a leather thong to a narrow paddle-shaped board. Hold-

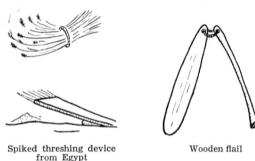

Spiked threshing device   Wooden flail
from Egypt

ing the sheaf to the floor with one hand, the farmer beat the seed heads in a downward-outward motion until he had knocked out all the grain. Not only the ingenuity of the farmer, but the type of grain to be threshed determined which of the threshing instruments would best serve its purpose (Is. 28:27-28).

Winnowing and Cleansing the Grain. — Whatever the mode of threshing, the process of winnowing or separating the chaff and bits of straw from the wheat remained practically uniform. The mixture was first shoveled and swept to one side of the threshing floor. Then the farmer took a long-handled broad wooden shovel or a close-pronged wooden fork and threw the chaff and grain up into the wind. The chaff and lighter waste matter blew to windward, while

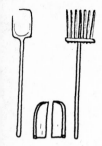

Winnowing "fans"

the wheat fell on a pile by itself. Illustrations on the Egyptian monuments show men with two short flat boards about 6″ by 14″ with which they dug into the pile of grain and chaff and then threw it backwards over their heads into the wind. This chaff, as comparatively worthless, was used for fuel or burned up in the fields, while the straw served as bedding and food for the animals in winter.

After repeating the winnowing process several times, the farmer completed the cleansing of the grain with a sieve (Luke 22:31; Amos 9:9). A sieve might be a copper bowl punctured full of holes through which dust and dirt could fall. It might consist of a pillbox-shaped container with its open bottom covered with a network of linen or fiber cords forming a close-meshed screen.

MEASURING, TRANSPORTATION, AND STORAGE OF GRAIN

The Measuring Process. — The measuring process was performed very carefully and ceremoniously with "good measure, pressed down, and shaken together, and running over" (Luke 6:38). The containers used for measuring were made of clay pottery, of copper, or of wood, in standard sizes convenient for handling. (See *Dry Measure,* Chap. VIII.)

Transportation and Storage of Grain. — After the measuring process the farmer loaded the grain into sacks or baskets, slung them over the backs of his donkeys, and took them to his home. His wife carefully washed the grain intended for household use and spread it out to dry in the sun on the flat roof or in the open courtyard. Then she might sift it once more before finally storing it away in large vermin-proof jars,

Storage jar and measure of pottery

or in bins of sun-baked clay bonded together with straw or woven fiber, until the family needed it for food — the "barrel" of the widow of Zarephath (1 Kings 17:12).

Spiritual Applications of the Harvest Processes. — Like so many processes of everyday life, the harvest finds its application in the spiritual realm. "The harvest is the end of the world; and the reapers are the angels" (Matt. 13:39). Again, John the Baptist describes the Messiah as a Thresher, giving His threshing floor its final, thorough cleanup of the season: "Whose fan (shovel) is in His hand, and He will thoroughly purge His floor and gather His wheat into the garner; but He will burn up the chaff with unquenchable fire" (Matt. 3:12; Luke 3:17). Jesus looked upon humankind of His own day as a "field white already to harvest" (John 4:35). It is a task, not for one, but for many workers. To His disciples of all ages He says, "The harvest truly is plenteous, but the laborers are few. Pray ye therefore the Lord of the harvest that He will send forth laborers into His harvest" (Matt. 9:37-38).

Pottery bin
or garner

REVIEW QUESTIONS AND EXERCISES

1. Discuss the relation of land ownership to the development of a settled and prosperous agriculture.
2. Describe the process of terracing a strip of Palestinian hillside. Use a diagram to illustrate your description.
3. Describe one irrigation device used in the ancient world.
4. Draw three types of yokes used for oxen. Which do you think would be the most effective?
5. Describe the construction and use of the plow. What additional process might be necessary in the preparation of the land for sowing?
6. Outline the process of cutting the grain, with a diagram of the instrument used. What was the purpose of binding the grain into sheaves? Explain the term "gleaners."
7. Give the reason for the usual location of the threshing floor, and explain its construction.

˙. Describe two or more methods of threshing the grain from the straw, with diagrams of the instruments used.

9. Why would the trodden-out grain need to be winnowed? Describe the instrument and the process employed in winnowing.

10. What were the methods used in
    a) measuring grain?
    b) transporting grain?
    c) storing grain?

PROBLEMS FOR FURTHER STUDY

1. Develop the thought in the glorified Savior's words to Saul of Tarsus, "It is hard for thee to kick against the pricks (goad)" (Acts 9:5). How might this passage be used in bringing the self-righteous critic of the church to his senses?

2. With the help of a commentary, study the Parable of the Four Kinds of Soil (Luke 8:5-15), with a view to presenting it to the Sunday school teachers or some church society. What encouragement does this parable offer for us not to become tired of our task of sowing or careless in our preparation if fine results do not show immediately? In this connection study the Parable of the Growth of the Seed (Mark 4:26-29), and note how much depends upon us and how much God Himself takes care of through the wonderful power He has put into the seed.

3. Apply to your own congregation and its called workers the passage "Thou shalt not muzzle the mouth of the ox that treadeth out the corn" (1 Cor. 9:9; 1 Tim. 5:18).

4. John the Baptist has left us a powerful description of the Savior's judgment of the world in Matt. 3 and Luke 3. Explain the whole passage with the proper applications.

5. The harvest of souls needs many workers. With the ancient agricultural processes as the model, picture the work of each member of your congregation in the preparation of the soil, the sowing, and the reaping. How much is God's work? How much does He delegate to us? (1 Cor. 3:6; Mark 4:26-29).

CHAPTER III

Vineyards and Orchards

The importance of grapes, olives, and other fruits in Palestinian life can scarcely be overestimated. Climate and soil were ideal for their culture. Where the rough nature of many mountain sections made it almost impossible to grow wheat or barley, a fig tree or two could take root and find nourishment. And over the stony hillsides, too barren even for sheep and goats to find food, grew great networks of grapevines, firmly rooted in some pocket of rich soil, hidden in a deep crevice of the forbidding limestone waste. In land too loose and sandy to insure a surface crop, the hardy and long-lived olive, striking its roots deep, defied the blazing sun of summer through year after year of drought. Besides furnishing food and drink to the people of Palestine itself, the vine and olive and other fruit trees supplied great quan-

Grapevine rooted in
a crevice

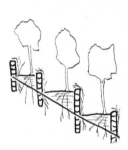

Cross section of a terraced
vineyard

tities of their products for export, in exchange for copper and iron, precious stones, spices and ointments, and other commodities.

BUILDING AND CARING FOR THE VINEYARD

Reclaiming the Hillsides and Planting the Vines. — Though grapevines grew wild in many sections of Palestine, the people were not satisfied with the wild variety or with the haphazard method of their growth on the mountainsides. Even at the time of the Hebrew conquest the land was covered with vineyards bearing clusters of grapes that amazed the spies of Moses sent in from the wilderness to reconnoiter (Num. 13:23-27). After the Israelites had occupied Canaan, they built up and expanded this industry. The care which they took of their vineyards is a symbol of God's care for Israel, His vineyard (Ps. 80:8-19).

As in the case of agriculture, the hillside often had to be cleared of stones and terraced so that sufficient soil could be found to nourish a full stand of grapevines (Is. 5:1-2; Micah 1:6). The choicest shoots were then planted. They were carefully pruned and cultivated and trained over the terrace wall or on trellises in the vineyard or about the home (1 Kings 4:25; Hos. 2:12).

The Care and Protection of the Vineyard. — After some years the vines were allowed to bear fruit, and with proper care and skillful cutting back or pruning of the too-luxuriant growth, they would continue to produce for many succesive years. In order to protect the vines from the "little foxes" and other marauders, the vineyard might be fenced in with

Watchtower in a vineyard   Grape cluster and   Ancient baskets
                                   pruning knife

a wall six or seven feet high and furnished with a tall watch-tower of stone in which the whole family might live during the harvest and from the roof of which they could carefully observe the maturing crop in order to guard it against marauders (Is. 5:1-7; Song of Sol. 2:15).

HARVESTING AND PRESSING THE GRAPES

The Grape Harvest. — In the month of June the grape harvest began. The bunches of grapes were cut off with knives or sickles (Rev. 14:14-20), gathered into large baskets, and taken at once on the backs of men or of donkeys to the wine press in order to extract the juice before decay or fermentation had set in.

The Construction of the Wine Press. — In the lower portion of the vineyard itself or in the valley beneath, the owner "digged his wine press," (Matt. 21:33). Quarrying out of the solid rock if possible, he cut a vat, roughly square or circular in shape, perhaps six to twelve feet in diameter and from one to two feet in depth, similar to the familiar wading pools in our parks. From this shallow depression a number of channels led through the rock to a deeper trough-like container quarried alongside, but at a lower level than the first.

The Use of the Wine Press. — Pouring the grapes into

Rock-hewn wine press
a) upper vat
b) lower vat
c) channel

the shallow upper basin to the depth of about a foot, the men tramped around and around in the slippery mass until they had reduced the grapes to a pulp and the juice flowed freely through the channels to the lower vat. Here the seeds and other solid matter gradually settled to the bottom. One of the workers then dipped off the juice into large jars or directly into wine skins, which he then loaded into carts or on the backs of donkeys and transported home.

The work of pressing grapes was, in itself, extremely tiring and disagreeable. Trudging in the yielding, slippery pulp, holding to the branches of a convenient tree or to each other's hands to keep from falling, the wine pressers lightened their burden by making a festival of the occasion. Accompanied by a piper who with inspiring music encouraged them to speed up their tempo, they literally danced about in the wine press, their quick steps making their tramping all the more effective. During the rest periods they refreshed their bodies with the fresh grape juice or with the wine of other years and their minds with conversation, riddles, and jokes.

Compare with this scene of enthusiasm and levity the

prophetic picture of the suffering Savior in Gethsemane, saying, "I tread the wine press alone" (Is. 63:3). There is no one to help Him. He tramples, but no one pipes a tune to His solitary labors. He takes with Him Peter and James and John, but repeatedly they fall asleep when He needs them most. The anguish, the bloody sweat, the scourging, and the crucifixion must be endured — alone. Alone He works out the salvation of the world.

Sack-type wine press

Other Methods of Extracting the Juice. — Other methods of pressing grapes were no doubt used in ancient Palestine. The Egyptian monuments show a sack filled with grapes hung horizontally in an upright wooden frame. By means of a stick inserted through the end of the sack the workers gradually twisted the sack until they had wound it up tightly, thus expelling all the juice. The modern Palestinians have a means of extracting the last of the juice from the solid matter in the wine press. They mix the pulp with clay until it forms a thick sticky mass, then they heap it up, bind it about with vines and fiber, and set a great flat stone upon the top of the pile. Upon this stone they exert additional pressure by throwing their own weight upon the end of a pole, hooked under a convenient rock, and resting upon the top of the stone. In the unchanging East it is quite likely that this method was also in use two thousand years ago.

Large storage jars for wine

WINE AND OTHER GRAPE PRODUCTS

The Process of Making Wine. — In the home the wine was allowed to go through its first process of fermentation, which ordinarily began within a few days. After several weeks they poured it off the lees or dregs (Is. 25:6) and allowed it to ferment again. Then they might place it in large jars of stone and store it until needed. More likely, however, they would use wineskins for this purpose. These are the "bottles" of the Bible. The Jew made his wine bottle of a goatskin, sewed together where it had been cut to remove it from the carcass, to form a sack which could be tied at the

neck and hung up. The resilience of the *new* rawhide took up whatever expansion might result from the process of fermentation. Of course, no one would think of putting "new wine into old bottles," since the old dried and cracked skins from the previous year were unsafe (Matt. 9:17). No doubt the ancient Biblical peoples sometimes made the wine bottles just as modern Mediterranean peoples often do — turning

Goatskin wine "bottle"

the hairy side of the goatskins inward so that the wine cured in the hair of the goat, thus deriving from its container a distinctive though, to us perhaps, not a very appetizing flavor.

What was left of the pulp after the juice had been pressed out might be put in a vat, covered with water, and allowed to ferment. The resulting product was a very poor grade of wine or vinegar (Ps. 69:21; Matt. 27:48).

Evaporation pan

Fresh Grape Juice and Grape Honey. — The Jews liked to drink *fresh* grape juice in season. On account of the hot climate and the lack of knowledge of fruit canning, which is part of every housewife's indispensable equipment today, the Jewish woman found it impossible to keep the juice in the fresh form for more than a few weeks at most. In order to preserve some of the fresh grape flavor, she placed the juice in large flat pans over a slow fire and boiled it down until it resembled a thick syrup. This was known as "grape honey," or simply "honey." Though some travelers have suggested that it was this type of honey that God meant when He spoke of "a land flowing with milk and honey" (Ex. 3:8), this interpretation seems far-fetched. The regular honey was certainly plentiful, especially in the wild and rocky sections of the country (Deut. 32:13; Matt. 3:4), and in the flower-covered Plain of Sharon. Without any further processing, the grape honey served throughout the year for sweetening, as a flavoring, and for the many confections prepared by the Israelites.

Fresh Grapes and Raisins as Food. — Ripe grapes were eaten *raw* throughout the summer season. Large blue grapes, similar to our Concord variety, were favorites (Gen. 49:11; Is. 5:2); but green, amber, and white ones also grew abundantly. In order to preserve fruit for the long winter and spring season, bunches of grapes were made into raisins. They were picked when not too ripe, dipped into a solution of lye to remove the waxy covering, dried on a flat rocky spot or on the clay housetops, then dipped in olive oil, drained again, and left in the hot sun until thoroughly dehydrated. Rich in vitamins and minerals, raisins filled an important requirement of ancient Palestinian diet (1 Sam. 25:18).

THE OLIVE AND OLIVE OIL

The Planting and Care of Olive Trees. — Olive trees flourished throughout Palestine in ancient times. The olive prefers a sandy, somewhat dry soil and will thrive where other fruit trees find difficulty in keeping alive. The Canaanite farmer had cultivated the olive long before the conquest, and when the Israelites under Joshua began to take over their inheritance, they found olive orchards already firmly established.

The olive is planted in the form of a shoot from a cultivated olive tree,

The growth of an
olive shoot

or it may be grown from seed and grafted with fresh twigs from an older tree. It grows very slowly, requiring years before it bears its first crop. However, it reaches an extremely old age, and by constant pruning and grafting its period of productivity may be extended almost indefinitely. Some olive trees in the Near East are said to be as much as 2,000 years old.

Pruning was done with saws and pruning hooks. The pruning saw of the ancient East, with its pistol-grip wooden handle and curved blade, was very much like our own. The Prophet tells his people to "beat their spears into pruning

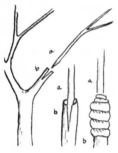

The grafting process
a) shoot
b) old branch

Pruning saw and
pruning hook

hooks" (Is. 2:4), hooked knives at the end of wooden handles by means of which smaller branches were cut off with a downward pull of the handle.

The Olive Harvest. — The olive harvest begins in August, when the fruit is just beginning to take on a whitish hue but is still quite firm. Since the olives are still firmly attached to the tree at this stage and hand picking would take too long, they are knocked from the tree with sticks. Thus the Hebrew word for "picking" olives really means "knocking." This process damages the twigs and branches to such an extent that the yield for the next year is spoiled, so that the farmer counts on a crop only every second year. Gathering the olives in baskets, the grower transports them, either slung across his own shoulders or on the back of a donkey, to the olive press.

Oil-Pressing Equipment. — Olive presses are of many varieties. The poorer people may simply use a somewhat concave face of the natural rock into which a few olives are placed at a time and then ground to a pulp with a stone held in the hand or rolled by hand over the fruit. Sometimes this process is carried on in the basin of the wine press. The most efficient method of extracting the oil is the olive mill, into the basin of which the olives are dumped in order to have a stone fixed

Ancient olive press

to a lever rolled around and around upon them until they are completely crushed. Several varieties of these mechanical mills are in use in Palestine, and the remains from ancient times show that the process in those days was very similar.

Grade of Olive Oil. — Whatever the form of the press, the operation produced almost immediate results in the clean flow of oil, very light and transparent, which was put by itself as a first-grade product. Before long the continued crushing would add the brownish tinge of broken pits and the green of olive skins to the oil until the last to be extracted might be very dull in color. The owner commonly kept this oil for use about his own household, since the better grades brought higher prices on the market. The last of the pulp might be put into a sack and fixed into a

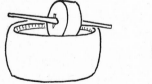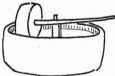

Ancient olive presses

wooden frame, where it received the final pressing to remove
the last bit of oil. From the olive press the olive oil was
taken in large pottery jars to the market or to the home.

Uses of Olive Oil. — It would be difficult to find a product
more indispensable to God's Old Testament people than
olive oil. They used it in the ritual of consecration to the
priesthood (Ex. 29:7) and the kingship (1 Sam. 16:13) as
well as in the sacrifices (Num. 28:28). It furnished the fuel
for lamps and torches (Ex. 27:20). They used it to anoint
the head after a day in the burning heat (Ps. 23:5; Luke
7:46). After bathing they anointed the body with it. They
put it on their wounds as a salve (Luke 10:34). In their
bread, their pastry, and especially in their fried foods, it

took the place of lard and butter and the
numerous vegetable fats and salad oils
familiar to us. Because they depended
so much upon this natural oil, a food,
an unguent, a medicine, and an internal
lubricant all in one, they probably spared
themselves some of the digestive dis-
turbances, bowel troubles, ulcers, and
cancers which our modern age seems

Horns of oil

to have accepted as inevitable. As it
was, there was plenty of sickness and contagion because of
the woeful lack of disposal facilities for garbage and sewage,
the swarms of flies, and the ever-present bacteria of the
unsanitary Eastern community environment.

Olive oil was not only used in the home, but was carried
by shepherds and travelers in containers made from the
hollow horns of animals, especially those of cattle and rams.

The olive symbolized national prosperity (Ps. 52:8).
Among all nations and at all times since the Flood it has
been an emblem of peace, just as the olive leaf which the
dove brought back to the ark (Gen. 8:11) proved that God's
anger had abated and that He was once more at peace with
the world.

OTHER COMMON FRUITS

The Fig Tree. — Among the most common of Palestinian fruits were the various kinds of figs. These flourished everywhere, in the open vineyard or near the house. Times of peace and plenty were pictured as "every man sitting under his own vine and under his own fig tree" (1 Kings 4:25; Micah 4:4). When God "smote their vines also and their fig trees," there was hunger and despair throughout Israel (Ps. 105:33; Jer. 5:17).

As winter approaches, the fig tree sheds its leaves and remains bare throughout the cold months. Rather late in spring the tips of the branches begin to thicken into globules, a few of which may ripen by the end of May. These are called the "hasty fruit" (Is. 28:4; Nah. 3:12). Though they are not of nearly as fine a quality as the later figs, they are eagerly awaited and considered a special delicacy because they are out of season (Jer. 24:2; Hos. 9:10). Meanwhile the regular yield of figs is slowly forming on the green shoots which have grown in spring. The harvest or summer fruit comes from about the end of July to the middle of August (Amos 8:1).

Fig branch and fruit

Besides the hasty fruit and the regular crop of figs, there are also occasionally "winter figs," which ripen very late in fall. People look forward to them just as they do to the hasty fruit, because they, too, are out of season. With its three crops of fruit, the fig tree bears nearly half of the time.

The fruit and leaves of the fig tree normally come at the same time, much later than the leaves of other trees. Thus a fig tree breaking out into full leaf is a sign that summer is now at hand (Matt. 24:32). Jesus cursed the fig tree, not because it failed to bear figs before the proper season, but because by sending forth the leaves it gave the impression that it was already bearing fruit. His curse is therefore a solemn warning against pretending to be what one is not (Mark 11:13-14, 20-21).

Figs furnished a palatable and very nutritious fresh fruit over a long season of each year. When they had been dried in the sun and packed away in pottery jars or in matted-together "cakes," they were available for food the year round (1 Sam. 25:18). Palestine produced so many figs that they were exported to Western nations.

The Prophet Amos mentions sycamore fruit (Amos 7:14). These figs are smaller and less tasty than the cultivated

The date palm

variety, but they still grow wild along the highways just as they did when Zacchaeus climbed up into one of them in order to see Jesus as He passed by at Jericho (Luke 19:4).

The Date Palm. — Date palms grew wild along the mild shore of the Mediterranean down towards the Egyptian border and in the tropical valley of the Jordan. Jericho, in the Jordan valley, somewhat north of the Dead Sea, was known as the "City of Palm Trees." Palms also grew plentifully along the fringes of the desert wherever a moist spot or a spring of water made an oasis. The date palm was one of the most valuable of all trees of the Near East, particularly in the desert region (Ex. 15:27). Travelers of all ages have depended upon this fruit, which they could pick and eat raw along the way. Like figs, dates were also dried and caked together for winter use.

Branches of palm trees were traditionally taken up to Jerusalem for the Festival of the Passover. These, as well as the branches which the people cut down from the trees along the way (Matt. 21:8; Mark 11:8), would be available to play a part in the royal welcome given to Jesus as He rode into Jerusalem on that first Palm Sunday (John 12:13).

Pomegranates. — The pomegranate tree is very much like our hawthorn or "thorn apple," but taller. The fruit is somewhat larger than an average apple. It has a sweet, tangy juice and somewhat reddish-purple seeds. It is often mentioned in the Old Testament (Hag 2:19; Deut. 8:8; Joel 1:12). Spiced wine was made from its juice (Song of Sol. 8:2). Golden bells, alternating with pomegranates of blue and purple and scarlet, decorated the hem of the high priest's robe used in the Tabernacle service in the wilderness (Ex. 28:33-34) and brass pomegranates adorned the pillars of Solomon's Temple (2 Kings 25:17).

The pomegranate

Almonds

Apples or Apricots, Peaches, and Citrus Fruits. — Apples are referred to in various passages (Prov. 25:11; Joel 1:12; Song of Sol. 2:3, 5), though some travelers think that these passages refer rather to apricots, which, with peaches and the citrus fruits, oranges and lemons, flourish throughout the mild Mediterranean region, though they are not mentioned in Scripture.

Nut Trees. — Among the very earliest trees to blossom in spring are the almonds, which seem to have always been plentiful throughout the Near East (Gen. 43:11; Ex. 25:33; Eccl. 12:5). They burst into bloom so suddenly as to be proverbial (Jer. 1:11). Walnuts are also common throughout Palestine. Shelled almonds and walnuts are mixed with dried raisins and figs and used at meals, and they are carried by shepherds and travelers for lunch along the way.

Oak trees were evidently very plentiful in Palestine. Rebekah's nurse was buried under an oak near Bethel (Gen. 35:8). Absalom caught his head in the thick boughs of a

great oak (2 Sam. 18:9). The fallen people of God carried on their adulterous worship among the oaks of the high places (Hos. 4:13). Like the cedars of Lebanon the oaks of Bashan were proverbial for their wood (Is. 2:13; Ezek. 27:6). Acorns from the oaks — and the pods, or "husks," of the carob tree, with their bean-sized dark-brown seeds — still fatten the herds of pigs raised by the Gentile inhabitants of Palestine, just as

'Husks" of the carob tree

they did in the days of the Prodigal Son and the unfortunate Gadarenes (Luke 15:16; 8:32).

REVIEW QUESTIONS AND EXERCISES

1. Why was Palestine peculiarly well adapted to the culture of grapes?
2. From Isaiah's description (Is. 5:1-7) show how a vineyard came into being.
3. Using a diagram, describe the construction of the wine press and its use.
4. Describe the method of fermenting and of storing the fermented wine in "bottles."
5. A large portion of the grape crop was used for wine. In which other ways did grapes furnish food and drink to Biblical peoples?
6. Describe the planting, growth, and general appearance of the olive tree. When and how were the olives harvested?
7. Illustrate at least one process of pressing the juice from the olives. Which olive oil was best? Why?
8. Name as many uses as you can for olive oil in the daily life of the ancient Near East.
9. Describe the fig tree and its fruit. How were the figs prepared for market?
10. Where was the date palm grown? How were dates prepared and preserved for use?
11. Name and briefly describe at least five additional varieties of fruit and nuts grown in the Holy Land.

PROBLEMS FOR FURTHER STUDY

1. Develop the thought of the passage Is. 63:1-6, showing how the statement "I tread the wine press alone" is true of Jesus in His state of humiliation as well as in His exaltation on Judgment Day.
2. "New wine in old bottles" (Matt. 9:17) — interpret this passage, using a commentary if necessary.
3. Why were the dried fruits so important to the health of people in ancient times? Try to find out their food value.

CHAPTER IV

Food and Drink

According to the Prophet Isaiah, bread and water are the "stay and staff" of life (Is. 3:1) — the two essentials without which God's people would perish.

The mountain ridge of Palestine is largely made up of limestone rock. Spongelike, its porous surface "drinketh water of the rain of heaven" (Deut. 11:11) during the wet winter seasons, building up a vast reservoir which makes possible "a land of brooks of water, of fountains, and depths that spring out of valleys and hills" (Deut. 8:7). Sometimes the water gushes forth as "a spring of water whose waters fail not" (Is. 58:11). In another place a well, dug deep, intercepts an underground stream, as at the famous Jacob's Well, where Jesus talked to the Samaritan woman (John 4:6). Where the natural springs and underground streams could not be found, the people of necessity dug holes into the ground or rock, making watertight containers by stopping the seams and cracks with pitch or by plastering the cistern wall from the inside. They then directed rivulets of rain water into these cisterns from the hillsides, much as we collect water from our roofs. If the rains were not abundant or the cistern sprang a leak and lost its contents by gradual seepage, their hopes were disappointed. The Lord, through Jeremiah, gives this familiar picture a spiritual interpretation when He says, "My people . . . have forsaken Me, the

Fountain of living waters, and hewed them out cisterns, broken cisterns, that can hold no water" (Jer. 2:13).

In times of prolonged drought people had to "drink water by measure" (Ezek. 4:16), and even "the nobles have sent their little ones to the waters; they came to the pits, and found no water; they returned with their vessels empty; they were ashamed and confounded" (Jer. 14:3). In the morning and again in the cool of sunset the women of the village gathered at the spring or cistern with their juglike earthenware pitchers, which they carried home upon their heads or shoulders. The "pitcher broken at the fountain" is to Solomon a symbol of death (Eccl. 12:6). Modern

A broken cistern

Cooling a jug of water

travelers say that a supply of drinking water is always kept in a container standing in the breeze at the window, where it will be kept cool by evaporation of the moisture exuded by its porous earthenware walls. The sick or restless kept a small cruse of water within easy reach at night, as did King Saul the night when David had him in his power and spared his life (1 Sam. 26:12-25). Just as we remember with gratitude some spring or well at home, so "David longed and said, Oh, that one would give me drink of the water of the well of Bethlehem which is by the gate" (2 Sam. 23: 15-16).

The other essential in the life of the ancient East is bread. "Want of bread" (Amos 4:6) is a description of famine, a time when people "eat bread by weight" (Ezek.

4:16), when "young children ask bread, and no man breaketh it unto them" (Lam. 4:4). Earthly prosperity, on the other hand, is pictured by "fullness of bread" (Ezek. 16:49). Let us see how the Israelites prepared this most important of foods.

PREPARING THE FLOUR

Grains Used for Flour. — Of the grains grown in the Holy Land, wheat was most commonly used for flour. Whereas barley was sometimes eaten by the poor, it was regularly fed to the domestic animals. Spelt, millet, and even lentils were sometimes ground into flour as an emer-

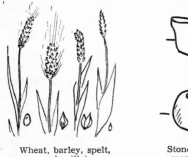

Wheat, barley, spelt, and millet

Stone flour grinder; mortar and pestle

gency food. (See the strange ingredients of Ezekiel's symbolic bread, Ezek. 4:9 f.)

Primitive Grinding Devices. — Perhaps the earliest of the flour mills consisted of a flat piece of rock on which a handful of wheat at a time was crushed and ground by a large stone held in the hand and rubbed back and forth over the kernels until they were reduced to flour. The grinder might kneel next to a flat-topped block of stone and vigorously push and then pull a heavy piece of stone, shaped like a loaf of rye bread, back and forth over the grain, using both hands with a vigorous motion like that of a woman at a scrubbing board. Such mills were used in ancient Egypt and may have been brought along to Palestine by the Israelites at the time of the Exodus. The Canaanite tribes still living in Palestine at the time of Saul and David used a rotary-type mill in which the cone of the upper millstone fit into a depression in the lower millstone. The grain was ground by twisting the upper stone back and forth under pressure from the palm of

the hand. The large mortar and pestle of stone, similar in shape to the small ones used by our druggists, did a fairly effective grinding job.

Construction of the Rotary Flour Mill. — All of these devices made very hard work of grinding, since they required continuous pressure, with either a rubbing motion to and fro or a twisting back and forth. They were superseded in most homes by

Canaanite mill

the rotary mill, still in use in its simpler form all over the Near East and among other backward peoples throughout the world. It consisted of two circular slabs of rock, one about 20 to 24 inches in diameter and 4 inches thick for the lower millstone, and another, slightly smaller and lighter, for the upper one. The lower millstone might be set into the earthen floor of the home so that it could not twist and turn. In a hole bored in the exact center of its upper surface, a round wooden plug was tightly wedged. From this plug a round iron bar projected upwards to form an axle of the upper stone. The upper stone had a four-inch hole cut through the center. Across this a strong piece of wood was wedged without completely filling the hole in the stone. Finally, a hole was drilled into this wooden crosspiece and the upper stone was slipped on to the axle fixed in the lower one. Near the outer edge of the upper stone a wooden peg protruded about six inches and served as a handle with which to turn the stone.

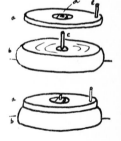

Rotary mill: (a) upper stone, (b) lower stone, (c) axle, (d) wooden bearing, (e) handle

Operation of the Rotary Mill. — In use the grinder turned the upper millstone with one hand, while she fed handful after handful of wheat into the central hole. As the wheat gradually worked its way downwards, the rotary motion drew it outwards between the stones, which crushed and ground it to pieces. Emerging as flour, it fell on a mat or on the floor all around the millstone. In order to make the flour easier to gather up, the lower millstone was sometimes fixed into a shallow pan of clay, re-enforced with straw or other fiber. This pan caught the flour as it fell. To lighten the burden of grinding, or for the sake of companionship, two women might grind at one mill, sitting cross-legged op-posite each other, so that one could push while the other pulled the mill-stone around (Matt. 24:41). Grinding flour was usually considered a menial task, the work of the housewife or of a maidservant (Ex. 11:5), a fact which gives point to the insult heaped upon Samson by making him, the noted strong man, do the work of a weakling (Judg. 16:21).

Mill set in a clay pan; flour sieves

Sifting the Flour. — As it came from the mill, the flour was carefully sifted to remove the bits of stone and other foreign substances as well as the coarse particles of grain. (For a description of sieves, see Chapter II, D.)

BREADMAKING AND OTHER BAKING

Preparing the Dough. — The grinding of flour, as well as the baking of bread, was usually a daily task ("our *daily* bread," Matt. 6:11) except on the Sabbath day, when, accord-ing to the Law of Moses, all unnecessary work ceased.

In making the bread, the housewife used flour, yeast, salt, olive oil, and water or milk. She made a thick batter of the flour and liquid, then added the previously soured yeast. The yeast might be made by adding a little sour milk to some flour and letting it stand in a warm place for sev-eral hours or overnight. Or a little dough, left from the previous baking, might serve to begin the souring process. The "leaven which a woman took and hid in three measures of meal until the whole was leavened" illustrates the quiet yet effective working of the Word of God in the hearts of men (Luke 13:21).   Only at religious festivals, or when in

great haste, did the Israelites eat their bread unleavened (Ex. 12:39, the Passover; Gen. 19:3, Lot). Its taste then resembled that of the wafer used in our Communion services. The mixing trough was a deep pan of metal or of pottery, its size depending upon the amount of dough to be mixed at a time. The consistency of the batter or dough varied according to the type of oven to be used in the baking process.

Simple camp oven

The Simple Camp Oven. — The simplest form of oven used in the camp or vineyard or on the road was a circular plaque of sheet iron, slightly convex, about 30 inches in diameter. This was greased with olive oil and held about eight or nine inches above the ground by three stones on which it rested. After a quick fire of twigs, straw, or dried animal dung had heated the plaque, the batter, about

Camp oven tied to camel pack

the consistency of that used for waffles or pancakes, was quickly poured out to a uniform crackerlike thickness over the surface of the plaque, where it stuck until it was baked through. The resulting thin sheet of bread might then readily be broken into pieces according to the family's needs. When the camp oven was not in use, it could easily be stored away or tied to the pack of a donkey or camel. Perhaps Sarah used such an oven when she baked the bread for her heavenly visitors (Gen. 18:6). It is still standard equipment in the camps of the nomadic races of the Near East.

Ovens Made of Clay. — Another type of oven consisted of a dome of clay, about three feet or more in diameter and perhaps half that height, built on the ground. It had a circular hole in the top, fitted with a stone lid. Small clean pebbles, scattered over the ground, formed the floor of the oven. The baker then made small roll-like loaves of leavened dough, allowed them to rise, and placed them upon the pebbles. She then replaced the lid and heaped fuel over the whole dome. Under the hot ashes left from the bonfire,

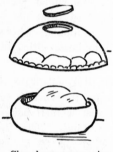
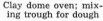

Clay dome oven; mixing trough for dough

Cylinder-style oven of clay

the dome and its contents reached the necessary temperature for slow, even baking. Then the baker raked away the ashes, took out the bread, put the lid back on, and covered the whole once more with the hot ashes to keep it warm for the next baking. Such an oven accommodated the baking of several families at one time.

Another common oven, still used in the Near East, was a cylindrical clay structure, about three feet high and two feet in diameter, covered by a lid. When a hot fire had been built and then allowed to smolder, small loaves were stuck to the inside surface above the live coals, where they were left to bake thoroughly. Perhaps Jesus had one of these two stoves in mind when He said: "If God so clothe the grass, which today is and tomorrow is cast into the oven, will He not also clothe you?" (Matt. 6:30.)

Sometimes a thin sheet of bread was stuck onto the sides of a circular hole in the earthen floor of the home, which formed the stove in the living room of a simple household. It was then baked by the heat of the coals smouldering in the bottom of this hole. Little loaves, or "cakes" of dough, might even be laid in the hot ashes or on the glowing coals themselves (1 Kings 19:6; John 21:9).

Community Ovens. — According to the Greek and Roman custom, many of the Jews of Jesus' time may have baked their bread in very large ovens which served the whole village, or bought it ready-baked from one of the master bakers, guilds of whom were to be found in the larger cities throughout the Roman Empire.

Oven in an earthen floor

Other Baked Goods; the Use of Honey. — Besides the various types of bread the Jewish women baked confections of many kinds. They had tarts of dough, folded up from the four corners over a handful of dried fruit or a quantity of thick grape honey. Ordinary honey was taken from the wild bees, which were very plentiful in Palestine, where they made their home in the rocks (Deut. 32:13), especially in the wilderness of the Jordan, where John the Baptist preached (Matt. 3:3-4). In the comb the Jews considered it a delicacy (Ps. 19:10; Is. 7:15). They also extracted it and stored it in earthenware jugs (1 Kings 14:3). As to its use, Solomon advises, "My son, eat thou honey, because it is good; and the honeycomb, which is sweet to thy taste" (Prov. 24:13), but he also warns that "it is not good to eat *much* honey" (Prov. 25:27). Evidently they used it chiefly as a sweetening in their various confections. They liked to make "cakes," more like our wafers or cookies, sweetened with honey, with which Moses compared the taste of the manna (Ex. 16:31). They had confections, similar to our doughnuts, fried in deep boiling olive oil. No doubt most of the other confections now baked in the Near East were also known in ancient times.

THE USE OF VEGETABLES AND HERBS

Gardening With and Without Irrigation. — Every Jewish village home had its kitchen garden, adjoining the house or at least close to it. Here were beds or rows of most of the herbs or vegetables found in our own gardens. On the outskirts of the larger cities truck gardeners grew quantities of vegetables for sale at the market places of the community. These larger gardens might be arranged in depressed beds so as to be accessible to an irrigation ditch. When he had flooded the ditch, the gardener passed along the row of beds, opening up a passage into each by means of a hoe or with his foot (Deut. 11:10). When that particular row of beds was full of water, he closed the passages, one after another, in the same way, and moved on to the next row. Though the early vegetables did well without irrigation,

Wooden irrigation hoe from Egypt

because of the moisture left in the soil by the spring rains, a second summer crop flourished only where irrigation could be provided. (For irrigation devices see Chapter II.)

The Legumes as Food. — Rich in protein and therefore a good hot climate substitute for meat, the legumes were extensively grown by the Israelites in all periods of their history. Beans of varieties similar to our own were raised in large quantities. At maturity the stalks were pulled up, put on piles, and allowed to dry thoroughly. They might then be threshed in the same way as grain on the threshing floor. (See Chapter II, D.) More likely, however, the farmer beat them out with a flail, consisting of a handle and a paddle-shaped blade, bound together by a thong of leather. He then winnowed the beans from the pods and straw, sifted them, and picked them over to get rid of the dirt and pebbles.

Taking them to his home in sacks or baskets, he spread them out on the housetop to dry very thoroughly, and then carefully packed them away in large earthenware jars or bins. Lentils, legumes which look like small split peas, are reddish

tan in color. Jacob used them to make the "red pottage" for a mess of which Esau was willing to sell his birthright (Gen. 25:34). They were also a favorite and very nourishing ingredient of soups and stews. The fitches, or vetch, mentioned in Is. 28:25, 27, have a round, black seed which is used chiefly as a flavoring material for stews.

Beans and lentils

Other Common Vegetables. — Melons and cucumbers grew in both Egypt and Palestine, but not in the dry wilderness of Sinai, where their lack added to the disgruntlement of the wandering Israelites (Num. 11:5). They were used as much as we use them today and added substantially to the hot weather diet. Wild gourds, though they smell like cucumbers, betray their poisonous nature by their bitter

Melons, gourd, and cucumbers

taste, and a stew containing them was recognized by Elisha's disciples as "death in the pot" (2 Kings 4:38-41).

Onions, garlic, and leeks have always been favorites of the Israelites. According to Easterners, they lose their strong taste when grown in extremely hot climates. Eaten raw with other foods, or cooked by themselves, or used as flavoring in the main dish of the meal, they supplied important

elements in the regular diet of the people. Parsley and celery were eaten raw or cooked with other foods (Num. 11:5). Lettuce and a species of cabbage were also eaten raw. Dill, mustard, and coriander seed provided strong flavoring. Cassia, or cinnamon bark, yields an oil which was used for flavoring (Ex. 30:24); as do mint and anise (Matt. 23:23) and saffron (Song of Sol. 4:14), which was used to flavor both food and wine.

The ancient world knew nothing of potatoes, one of the mainstays of our menus today.

Vegetable Stew. — A favorite dish for the main meal of the day was a thick stew made of a combination of many vegetables. It might have a base of beans, or lentils, with onions, garlic, celery, parsley, or other herbs and spices added. It might have lumps of dough, or dumplings, which helped to thicken it. It might contain small quantities of meat, fowl, or fish, which would thus be "stretched" to their full food and flavor value.

Dish of vegetable stew

Served in a large central dish or basin, the stew was taken with the hand or on a piece of the crackerlike bread, which thus served as a spoon until soaked and soggy, when it, too, could be eaten. If the host or head of the family wanted to convey a special mark of favor on anyone, he personally chose out the best morsels of meat or other food from the dish and put them into the mouth of the guest with his own fingers.

THE USE OF MEAT

General Economy in the Use of Meat. — The best meat was always scarce in Palestine in ancient times, as it still is today. Once a farmer had killed a cow, he lost his source not only of milk but of power for his plow or threshing machine as well. If he killed a sheep or a goat, he lost his source of wool and milk. Unless he wished to provide a very great feast, he would scarcely kill the fatted calf, as the father did on the Prodigal Son's return (Luke 15:23). The lamb without blemish had to be saved up until the time of the Passover Festival, when every morsel had to be eaten, even though several families had to go together to do it (Ex. 12:

3-10). Unless he cared to dry his meat in the not sun, as was done in the Bashan cattle country, or pack it in salt or salt brine, he had no way of preserving it for more than a few days at most, since refrigeration and safe canning methods were unknown.

Stewed Meats. — The use of small quantities of meat, fowl, or fish to flavor vegetable stew has been mentioned in the previous section. Meat might also be stewed in water in a pot over the fire, flavored to taste with various herbs and spices, perhaps also with dumplings added. A calf or kid might be stewed or "seethed" in milk, but the Old Testament ordinances forbade seething it in its own mother's milk (Ex. 23:19). Since stewing provides comparatively large quantities of broth or gravy and also makes use of the nutritive value in the joints and marrow, it is still a favorite way of preparing meat in the Near East.

Roasting a kid whole

Roasted Meats. — On very special occasions, such as one of the religious festivals, particularly the Passover, or when a long-absent relative returned home (Luke 15:23), or a prominent guest, or a whole visiting tribe was to be entertained, a calf, kid, or lamb might be served (Gen. 18:7). The method used was similar to the well-known barbecue of today. The animal was skinned and dressed and the meat seasoned and salted. A straight green pole, cut from a tree, was then arranged to pivot on two rocks or forked sticks at either side of an open fire. Inserting the pole the whole length of the animal next to the inside of the spine, the cook bound the sides of the carcass and its legs around the pole so that it was as nearly as possible of uniform thickness on all sides. The fire meanwhile had become a glowing bed of charcoal. Then the pole with the meat was arranged before the fire so that the drippings could be caught in a pan beneath. After several hours of roasting, the meat was removed and cut or torn into pieces as suggested by the various joints. The best pieces then became the portion of various guests in the order of their importance socially or of the favor which the host wanted to bestow upon them.

Fish. — Fresh fish were cut open and cleaned, seasoned, and roasted over the glowing coals of a wood fire (John 21:9-13), until they formed a crisp morsel which could be held in the hand to be eaten (Mark 8:7). Fish might also be dried on the hot sands of the beach, salted, turned over and salted again and again, until thoroughly dried. They could then be kept for some time without spoilage. At times these dried fish were ground into "fish flour," which was then carried in the pouch of the traveler or shepherd to serve as lunch.

Roasting fish

Fish is one of the best hot-weather meats. The Israelites learned to love it as a food in Egypt, and during their forty years stay in the wilderness they longed for the days when they had plenty of it (Num. 11:5). Along the shores of the Mediterranean, along the Jordan River, and particularly the Sea of Galilee, where many families made their living by fishing (Matt. 4:18-21), fish were always available and comparatively cheap.

Fowl. — In a country where meat was so scarce that two sparrows were sold for a farthing (Matt. 10:29), and other birds were allowed for food, except those specifically forbidden in the Law (Lev. 11:13-19), it was natural that fowl would be domesticated. Chickens are not mentioned directly in the Old Testament and only incidentally in the New, where Jesus refers to a hen and her chickens (Matt. 23:37), and Peter is warned by the crowing of a cock in or near the courtyard of the high priest's palace (John 18:27). However, they were raised so extensively in the countries bordering on the Holy Land that the same is no doubt true of Palestine itself. Wild fowl of various kinds were also plentiful throughout the region. Among the smaller birds various types of doves were especially prized on account of their fine flavor. The poor used them as substitutes for the usual lamb or kid in certain sacrifices (Luke 2:23-24). The methods of preparing fowl by roasting and stewing were

similar to those used in the preparation of meat and fish.

Eggs provide a good source of protein in a country where meat is scarce. To Job the tastelessness of egg white is proverbial (Job 6:6). Isaiah mentions the gathering of eggs (Is. 10:14), and Jesus speaks of a son asking his father for an egg (Luke 11:12). No doubt the Israelites used eggs just as extensively as did the neighboring nations.

Ancient kitchen utensils

MILK AND MILK PRODUCTS

Source of the Milk Supply. — A plentiful supply of milk typified the prosperity of ancient Canaan, the Land of Promise, for God's people (Ex. 3:8). The shepherd out on the hills depended largely on the milk of his flock for his daily food, for "who feedeth a flock and eateth not of the milk of the flock?" (1 Cor. 9:7.) He used the milk of the sheep as well as that of the goats (Deut. 32:14; Is. 7:21-22). Village families who could not have large flocks might still raise a few goats in order to have their own milk supply. The ranches of the East-Jordan Gilead and Bashan country practically lived on the milk of their herds of cattle, as nomadic peoples always have. Families in the settled areas might have a cow, which, besides doing some of the heavy work, furnished milk (1 Sam. 6:7) and milk products for them and their neighbors. City dwellers, on the other hand, particularly the poor, must have faced the same scarcity of good milk that has handicapped the people of slum areas ever since.

Uses of Milk. — Fresh raw milk furnished an important item in the diet of the village family and was used as a beverage at meals (Gen. 18:8), especially by young children (Heb. 5:12-13) and the sick. It was kept in jars immersed in cool springs of water or in the depths of limestone caves. Soured and thickened to the consistency of custard, it was considered a delicacy, as it still is among all peoples of the Near East. Commentators have suggested that this soured milk was what Jael "brought forth for Sisera in a lordly dish" (Judg. 5:25).

Cheese Making. — Soured milk can be made into cheese, many varieties of which seem to have been known to the Israelites. Cottage cheese was most easily prepared, palatable, and nutritious. Dehydrated, in the form of tough curds, it found its way into the shepherd's lunch along with dried fruits and nuts. The cottage cheese might also be pressed into lumps the size of a large ball, dropped into boiling water, then allowed to age. Such may have been the "ten cheeses" which Jesse sent with David when he went to see his brothers (1 Sam. 17:18).

Goatskin churn

The many other varieties of homemade cheese, quickly made out of sour milk or aged through a number of processes, have continued in use in the Near East and in southeastern Europe, no doubt in much the same form as they were used in Bible times.

Buttermaking. — Butter is mentioned in Gen. 18:8, where Abraham entertained the Angel of the Lord and His companions. It was made of cream, skimmed off the top of soured milk. The fat cells were broken down by churning a quantity of it (Prov. 30:33) back and forth on the knees, in a jug or other container, until the butter formed little lumps floating in the buttermilk. One of the devices used by modern Arabs may well be the same as that used nearly 4,000 years ago by Abraham. It consisted of a goatskin "bottle," made up in the same way as the wineskins, mentioned in Chapter III. Half filled with sour cream, it was then inflated with air to make it comparatively rigid and suspended by the legs of the goatskin so that it could swing freely from a tripod support made of sticks. The housewife jerked it back and forth by means of a rope attached to the neck of the bottle until the agitation produced the butter. As in many other cases of food preparation, this method of preparing butter was, to say the least, unsavory.

Butter, boiled down to remove the water and impurities, was stored in jars and used in the preparation of baked goods, in frying, and for various other cooking purposes. There is no evidence that it was used on bread as we use it today. Buttermilk, the by-product of buttermaking, furnished a refreshing and nourishing drink for the family.

Importance of Milk and Milk Products — In a country as hot as Palestine, particularly on the fringe of the desert, milk and milk products were vital to the life and health of the inhabitants as their chief supply of protein, calcium, and fat. Fresh milk, sour milk, and buttermilk provided a pleasant variety of refreshing beverages. Butter and the many varieties of cheese helped greatly in balancing and diversifying an otherwise limited diet. "A land flowing with milk . . ." (Ex. 3:8) helped to guarantee a physically strong and sturdy race.

REVIEW QUESTIONS AND EXERCISES

1. Using diagrams, describe two early methods of grinding flour before the rotary millstone came into use.
2. Describe a rotary mill. What were the advantages of this mill as compared with those described in Question 1? On a diagram note
    a) the lower millstone
    b) the upper millstone
    c) the axle
    d) the handle
3. What is leaven? Describe its use in the process of bread-making.
4. Outline the process of baking bread on a metal camp stove. Describe one type of clay oven.

5. Which legumes did the Israelites use for food? List some of the characteristics of legumes as to
   a) appearance
   b) food value
6. What are some of the ingredients you might expect to find in a stew prepared in an Israelite household?
7. Describe with diagrams one method of roasting meat. Why did the average Israelite family seldom have roast meat?
8. Enumerate four ways in which milk was used. Describe an Eastern method of making butter, using a diagram if you can.
9. Describe two methods of preparing fish as food.
10. What kinds of fowl were available to the Israelites as food? How was the fowl prepared?

PROBLEMS FOR FURTHER STUDY

1. Find as many similarities between the action of leaven and of the Word of God as you can. Apply them to your own method of teaching God's Word.
2. List the various foods that the average Israelite village family, with no canning process to depend on, might have in each of the four seasons of the year.
3. Summarize the information given by the Law of Moses regarding clean and unclean foods of
   a) animals
   b) birds
   c) fish
   d) insects
   List a few of the creatures mentioned in each category.

CHAPTER V

The Home and Its Furnishings

No particular type of dwelling is confined to any period in the history of Bible people. The construction of the home, as well as the luxury or poverty of its furnishings, varied with its location, the climatic conditions, the availability of building materials, and the occupation and comparative wealth and culture of the owner. Some houses served as dwelling places for many generations; others lasted only for a single season.

PRIMITIVE HOMES

Caves. — The limestone mountain ridge of Palestine is honeycombed with caves, large and small. From ancient times these have served as the homes of shepherds and their flocks and as refuges for exiles, such as Elijah (1 Kings 19:9) or David and his band when they fled before Saul (1 Sam. 24:3) or the 100 prophets whom Governor Obadiah hid by 50's in a cave to protect them from death at the hands of Ahab and Jezebel (1 Kings 18:4). Caves provided shelter for the poor and outcasts and lepers. Often they were the last home of the dead (Gen. 25:9; 49:29). Many houses consisted of a cave reaching back into the rock and one room

A booth of branches

or more, built of stone, in front of the cave opening. The winter offered no heating problem, since the caves always remained at a moderate temperature in the winter, and in the heat of summer were agreeably cool and pleasant.

Booths of Branches. — A seasonal shelter, but scarcely a suitable year-round home, was the booth made of tree branches put together in various ways. As a watchman's booth on top of the tower in the vineyard, it consisted of four upright poles connected by cross branches and covered with a network of twigs and leaves or grass to keep out the hot sun. Near the threshing floor a booth might be such a framework covered with straw. The roofs were flat, since they were not intended to keep out rain, but the rays of the sun only. At the Feast of Tabernacles the whole nation traditionally moved out into such temporary homes in commemoration of the time when Israel dwelt in booths (Lev. 23:42; Neh. 8.14).

Mud and Reed Huts. — In the Valley of the Nile, and undoubtedly also in the tropical valley of the Jordan River, temporary dwellings were constructed of river reeds, woven basketlike to form the walls, which were then plastered inside and out with mud from the river's bank. The roof was covered with rushes. Although these houses were very flimsy, they served well the temporary purpose for which they were built. When the flood season swept away the home, as it often must have done, the owner had few regrets, since he could easily build another of the same kind.

Kinds of Tents. — From the time of Jabal, who "was the father of such as dwell in tents and have cattle" (Gen. 4:20), nomadic peoples have traditionally used tents as the best means of providing portable protection from the sun and wind-driven dust as well as from the cold of the desert

Woven reed hut plastered
with mud

Small shelter tent

night. Ancient tents seem to have been very much like those in use in the deserts of today. A favorite material for the weaving of tent cloth was goat hair or camel hair, and the favorite color was black (Song of Sol. 1:5) or dark brown, in order to keep out the glare and reflection of the desert sun. Millions of tiny pin points of light showed through the loose weave, but when it rained, the taut cloth shrank and became waterproof.

A small shelter tent no larger than a blanket might be pitched by a lone traveler to protect him from the sun by day and from the moon by night. Larger tents housed a whole family, while very large ones sheltered several families or a whole clan. The front wall of most tents was so arranged that it could be held up on poles to form a sort of porch roof or awning during pleasant weather, while it could easily be lowered in the face of an approaching storm and pegged down securely to weather the blast. It could also be closed at night to shut out the cold. During their forty years of wandering in the desert the Israelites lived in

Family tent, closed

tents, and their portable house of worship was an elaborate tent in which God Himself deigned to dwell (Ex. 40:34).

The Large Tent and Its Furnishings. — The usual tent of desert dwellers was very large, with at least two central poles called "pillars" (Ex. 26:32). The roof of the tent sloped from the ridge to within three or four feet of the ground. Here it was held in place by cords (Jer. 10:20), tied to stakes (Is. 54:2) firmly driven into the ground with a wooden hammer. Jael drove such a tent pin through the temple of Sisera in order to rid Israel of the oppressor (Judg. 4:21). Between the two central poles a strip of tent cloth divided the quarters of men from those of the women. Along this cloth partition were piled the household supplies and baggage.

Large Bedouin tent

Ancient lamps

In the twilight of the tent's interior a lamp might be necessary even during the day. These were made of pottery or of brass in shapes ranging from a simple shell-like dish to a very elaborate one, shaped like a teapot or a gravy bowl. A lamp could be "set on a candlestick," or a pedestal (Luke 8:16), or hung from one of the main tent poles so as to light up the whole interior of the tent. (Bible people did not use wax or tallow candles as the King James version reads in the above passage.) A cotton or linen wick, immersed in the olive oil within the container, stuck out of the spout and burned very much like the wick of a candle or kerosene lamp. Since no glass protected the flame, the light flickered and wavered with every breeze. When the oil ran low, the wick smouldered and sputtered. Isaiah uses this picture to illustrate God's mercy when he says, "The smoking flax shall He not quench" (Is. 42:3; Matt. 12:20). On the floor were mats and rugs of various sizes and texture, depending upon the wealth of the owner. Rolled up and stored along the edges of the tent, the blankets and other bedding

A brazier

served as couches by day, while, with the rugs and mats, they provided beds at night. A small brazier for the charcoal fire, the stone mill, the kneading trough, the pots and other cooking utensils, the bins and jars and baskets of food completed the furnishing of the tent.

THE SIMPLE HOUSE

Building Materials. — The building material used in the common home varied with the locality in which it was built. In the rocky sections of Palestine proper the houses were constructed of the random pieces of limestone rock or large stones picked up in the fields, bonded together with mortar, made of burned slaked lime and sand. Along the Mediterranean, or in other sections of the country where rock was not so plentiful and had to be hauled long distances, the material usually used was clay. This was also the case in the Tigris-Euphrates valley, the ancient Plain of Shinar, where in connection with the tower of Babel we are told: "They had brick for stone, and slime (asphalt) had they for mortar" (Gen. 11:3). Adobe houses, similar to those of our own Southwest, were built in the plains of Syria and Mesopotamia.

Foundations and Walls. — Since there is never any sustained period of freezing weather, not even in the mountains of Palestine, it was not necessary to dig down "below the frost line," as we must do when we wish to erect a permanent building. This simplified the construction. The builder merely chose a level site or leveled a site with shovel and mattock. Careful to place his building above the flood level of a neighboring watercourse, he preferred to give it a solid footing on rock rather than on ground or sand (Matt. 7:24-27). Carefully measuring out the size of the structure on the leveled ground, he troweled a layer of plaster or clay where the walls were to be, and then laid the stone into the soft mortar, carefully filling the spaces between the stones with mortar. At the corners he placed large stones, preferably square, to serve as guides by which he was able to keep a straight row of stones, and eventually a straight wall. Thus he laid up layer upon layer of stone, careful to avoid getting one joint exactly above another. In the openings which formed the door and the windows, he built up squared masonry sides or inserted a framework consisting of sideposts and lintel and sill, which he then built into the wall.

Wall construction showing cornerstone, lintel and sideposts, "head of the corner"

Above the lintels the wall continued for a few more layers. Then the builder laid four or five heavy roof beams across from wall to wall and built them into the masonry. Upon these beams, consisting of poles perhaps six inches in diameter, the structure of the roof itself rested. In the center of the house he might set a post on which to rest a heavy crossbeam to help support the other beams.

Door, latticed windows, and roof construction

Doors and windows. — The door

openings were about six feet in height and perhaps two and a half feet wide. They were closed with doors made of wooden beams or heavy planks and hinged so as to swing freely. The doors were held shut by a bar or bolt which slid into place and might be opened or locked by a key inserted into a keyhole in the door or in the wall. Keys from the ancient world were very large compared with ours and had a number of fingers or hooks which fit into openings in the bar (Song of Sol. 5:4). Doors of the more pretentious homes were made of heavy wood, studded with brass or iron nails or even covered over with a coating of sheet metal. In the finest of homes and in palaces they might be made of solid slabs

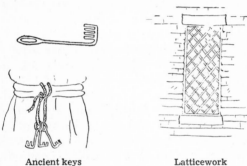

Ancient keys   Latticework

of stone with projections above and below on one side which fit into depressions in the sill and in the lintel so that the door could swing on these pivots.

The window openings, high up in the walls and very narrow so as to keep out possible robbers, might be left uncovered except for wooden bars and draperies so arranged as to cover the opening in cold or inclement weather at night. Usually, however, the windows were fitted with latticework of wooden slats set crisscross in a frame to fit the opening. While shutting out the vision of passers-by, this arrangement enabled the people inside to get the advantage of the summer breeze and to look out without being seen. Thus Solomon looked through his lattice to observe the life of the city and gather material for his proverbs (Prov. 7:6). Since the windows of the upper levels had no bars, Eutychus could fall out of the third-story window while listening to one of St. Paul's sermons (Acts 20:9-12; see also Josh. 2:15).

Construction and Use of the Roof. — The walls were continued upward to the tops of the roof beams, then the roof itself was laid. Smaller branches of trees were arranged crosswise over the heavy beams, then other branches were laid across these, then a layer of rushes or straw. Now the builder shoveled wet clay in a thin layer over the straw and tramped it solid. More branches were laid in the clay,

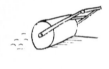

more straw, and more clay, then more branches, continuously crisscrossing the material until the roof had reached a thickness of a foot or more. Now it was allowed to settle and dry out. Finally a very smooth layer of pure clay, like the finish of a tennis court, was carefully put on to the depth of an inch or two, worked to a smooth finish, and left to bake in the sun.

Roof roller; cross section of roof

Such a roof needed constant care. After every rain it had to be rolled with a small stone roller which was always left on the roof for that purpose. Depressions had to be filled in with clay, and leaks needed to be repaired at once, or the whole roof might cave in during a rain, with a deluge of water and mud and broken sticks and straw falling down into the house.

The wall itself was continued above the roof line to form a parapet about three feet high. Either such a parapet or a solid rail had to surround the roof for the protection of those on it. This is a direct command of the Mosaic Law (Deut. 22:8). The top of the parapet was then finished with smooth clay, allowed to bake in the sun, and the roof was ready for occupancy.

In order to reach the roof, a stairway of stone or of brick, with carefully smoothed steps and a rail, was raised from street level to roof line. Or a stairway might be built inside the house, emerging at one corner of the roof where the walls extended upward and forming a penthouselike structure from which the family stepped out onto the roof.

Another type of roof used in the Near East today, and perhaps in the time of Jesus, has an arched or domed structure of stone which supports the weight of the clay above. These domed roofs are familiar to all of us through pictures of the Near East. No doubt they developed from the round

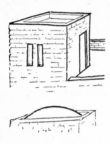

Enclosed stairway open-
ing on roof; domed roof

Open stairway and
upper room

arch and the cylindrical and domed construction of the Romans. Travelers have noted that many modern houses do not have the "battlement," or parapet, commanded by the Mosaic ordinances.

The roof of the Palestinian home was a very useful place. It served as a quiet spot for rest and prayer (Acts 10:9), a place to entertain visitors, to dry fruit and grain and flax and fuel, and to do other work (Josh. 2:6). In general it was a very convenient extension of the house itself.

Extra Rooms. — Though simple houses were usually only of one story and perhaps of one room, an upper room might be built at one side of the building by extending the outer walls upward and adding inner walls resting on supports beneath the roof reaching to the ground level. Like the roof itself, this upper room might be used by the family as a place for meditation and prayer or for rest. It might also be rented out for special occasions, such as the Feast of the

Passover or whenever crowds of people thronged into the city. In an upper room Jesus ate the Passover meal and instituted the Lord's Supper (Mark 14:15). In such a room, too, the disciples congregated for fear of the Jews and met their risen Lord (Acts 1:13). In villages the upper room might serve as a guest room for visiting relatives or notables. Thus Elijah lived in such a room in the home of the widow of Zarephath (1 Kings 17:19). In order to have a place for Elisha to stay, the Shunammite woman begged her husband, "Let us make a little chamber . . . on the wall; and let us set for him there a bed and a table and a stove and a candlestick" (2 Kings 4:10). Faithful Dorcas' body was reverently laid in an upper chamber until the Apostle Peter raised her from the dead (Acts 9:36-41). A second room on the lower floor level might serve as a shop for the head of the household to carry on his trade as carpenter, potter, weaver, or metalworker (see Chapter VI).

Another type of house had one very large room with a sort of mezzanine floor running along one side, supported by posts or arches of stone. On this upper floor level the family lived. Beneath it they kept their sheep and goats in winter. In the taller part of the house there was head room for a donkey, a cow, or perhaps even a camel. Overhead, on the rafters, hung the many useful articles of food and equipment described in the next section.

FURNISHINGS OF THE HOME

Utility in Preference to Beauty. — In a one-room house, occupied by a large household for living room, dining room, bedroom, and even for a workshop, there could be little chance of avoiding a cluttered-up appearance. To the comparatively poor family, however, such crowding denoted wealth in this world's goods, for everything in the room served one or more useful purposes and was immediately available when needed. Thus beauty and symmetry gave way to utility. The house was a home and workshop for the family, not a showroom for visitors.

Mats, Rugs, Beds, and Chairs. — Mats and rugs, woven

of wool, grass, straw, or other fiber, littered the floor by day, but they furnished a welcome protection against the cold hard clay of which it was composed. If desirable, they could be rolled up during the day and laid along the side walls or stored, with the bedding, in convenient shelves or niches in the walls. At night they took the place of mattresses for the whole family, while the hard floor itself served as bedstead and springs. Wealthy homes might have couches and beds, consisting of a framework of wood,

with legs about two feet long. A network of rawhide or cords stretched across the framework held a sort of heavy mat or mattress.

In the wealthier homes, chairs and stools of many types were used, but in the simple home, and in the tent of the Arab, cushions of various sizes, or the mats themselves, took the place of chairs.

Ancient couch, chair, and stool

Stoves and Braziers. — In the center of the room stood the metal brazier or stove. It might be made of iron or of brass, consisting of three legs riveted to one or two circular hoops of metal so that a small fire could be built below and a pot or pan set on the upper hoop above the flames. The fuel used was straw, brushwood (thornbushes, Is. 33: 12), charcoal, or, more likely, dried animal dung, carefully picked up in the fields and stored in heaps outside the home for winter use. This fuel, the same as the so-called "cow chips" of certain poor agricultural sections of our country today or the "buffalo chips" of our prairie pioneers, burns very much like charcoal with a clean, hot, almost smokeless flame.

Instead of a metal brazier, the stove might be a circular hole cut out of the solid earthen floor and lined with stones or plastered with clay, which then baked hard in the fire. Cooking utensils could be held over the fire by suspending them from a tripod or setting them on bars laid across the top of the hole.

Cooking Utensils. — Cooking utensils closely resembled those of our European ancestors as well as those in use in most primitive civilizations. Pots of various sizes, hammered out of sheet copper or brass, were fitted with heavy metal handles so that they could be hung over the fire. Pans of many shapes and sizes were also beaten out of copper. Long-handled copper ladles and spoons, as well as "flesh hooks," or forks, were used to stir the contents of the pots. Knives, made of bronze or iron in a variety of

Cooking utensils; ladle, spoon, pan, kettle, and basin

shapes and sizes, were fitted with wooden handles and served numerous purposes.

Many of the household utensils were clay pottery of simple rough texture or glazed by a second firing. Pottery jugs, with handles or without, served as containers for milk and water, olive oil and wine, as well as for the syrups made of grapes, figs, and dates. Many types of pitchers, cups, small deep saucers, and other kitchenware were made of glazed or unglazed pottery. In order to keep the dishes clean, they were carefully washed, wiped, and turned upside down (2 Kings 21:13).

Solving the Storage Problem. — Very large pottery jars or boxlike clay bins, holding up to three or four bushels, stored wheat to be ground into flour for family use. Somewhere on the floor there was room for the flour mill, an indispensable part of the equipment of every household, which no one was allowed to take in pledge, since the life of the family depended on it (Deut. 24:6).

In such a crowded home, no wonder the woman of the parable had to "light a candle and sweep the house and search diligently" among the mats and rugs, the bins and utensils of all kinds, the fuel for the fire, and the dust of the earthen floor itself, until she found her lost piece of silver. (Luke 15:8-10).

If the floor and walls were cluttered up almost beyond description, so was the ceiling. The crossbeams of the roof made covenient supports on which to hang the wineskins, "bottles in the smoke" (Ps. 119:83), in which the family's supply of this necessary beverage was stored. Large rings of onions and garlic, bunches of dried raisins, sheaves of dried dill and mint, and other aromatic herbs hung up out of the way, still within instant reach when needed.

Herbs, onions, and "bottles in the smoke"

In this crowded home the Jewish housewife, poor or well-to-do, spent nearly all of her time, taking care of her children, preparing her meals, doing her spinning and weaving and sewing and patching (Prov. 31:10-31). Only during her daily chore of grind-

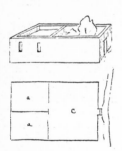
House with walled courtyard garden
(a) rooms, (c) court

ing flour outside her doorstep, or while enjoying her morning and evening trips to the village well to draw water for the family's use, would she get a chance to get outside and enjoy a chat with the other women of the village.

The Hebrew home was a closely knit family group whose parental love and filial respect and obedience might well serve as a model for many an outwardly Christian home of today.

LARGER HOUSES

Homes with Walled Gardens. — The simple house described above, or its expansion by the inclusion of an upper room or adjoining shop, was the usual home of the villager and the trade class of the cities. The well-to-do city dwellers demanded more pretentious homes. In some of these the rooms opened on a walled-in-garden with kitchen vegetables and herbs, a few fruit trees, and a grapevine with its arbor or trellis. A balcony, reached by a stairway from the garden, led to rooms on the second story. Comparatively bare and forbidding on the outside, with windows narrow and high up in the walls and accessible only by one street door, the home was very pleasant on the inside, with its fine view from all rooms into the landscaped central courtyard.

Homes Built Around a Courtyard. — Instead of mere walls surrounding the three sides of the garden space, a very large house might be built in the form of a hollow square so that the garden space became a courtyard completely surrounded by rooms opening onto it from all sides. In this case the courtyard itself was slightly sunken, with part of

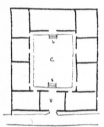

it paved and the rest devoted to garden vegetables and fruit trees. Around the inside of the courtyard ran a porch, reached by several low stairways. On the porch level the doors led into the various rooms.

Because all rooms fronted inwards toward the spacious courtyard, large houses could be built tightly against each other on both sides and at the back, and right up against the street line in the front, and still have an open sunny space within, with complete privacy for the

Floor plan of a house with central courtyard: (v) vestibule (c) court, (s) steps

family. Sometimes these houses had two or more stories, with the porches supported on posts, reached by stairways extending upward from porch to porch. The flat roof over all the rooms could still be used for the many purposes to which it was devoted in the simpler houses.

Just as in some of our business blocks it is possible to step over the parapets from roof to roof, so Jesus advises his hearers to flee over the housetops of Jerusalem in order to escape from the city when the long-threatened destruction finally comes upon it (Mark 13:15).

Palaces of the Nobles and Priests. — As the nation prospered, the wealthy and influential vied with each other in building mansions and palaces suitable to their exalted station. The houses of David and Solomon served as patterns of luxury which the later kings strove to exceed and which the nobles and the wealthier priests were quick to imitate (Is. 28:7-8). Spacious palaces of cut stone and marble (Amos 5:11), beamed with cedar overlaid with gold, were rightly viewed with alarm by the inspired Old Testament Prophets as signs of worldliness, altogether incompatible with true devotion to the Lord (Amos 6:8-14; Hos. 4:6).

Built into these palaces were luxurious fountains and baths, patterned after those of Egypt and Babylonia and, in later Judea, after those of Greece and Rome. Couches of ivory (Amos 6:4), priceless rugs and draperies of the finest imported silk, alabaster containers for precious ointments brought from the far corners of the world, were the setting for the luxurious and wanton parties and feasts put on by the wealthy Israelites (Is. 28:7). In such a home in New Testament times the rich man could clothe himself in purple and fine linen and fare sumptuously every day, scarcely conscious of poor Lazarus, who lay at his gate, full of sores and desiring to be fed with crumbs which fell from the rich man's table (Luke 16:19-21).

The homes of the wealthy, often built with money gained by grinding the faces of the poor and devouring widows' houses (Is. 3:15; Matt. 23:14), encroached upon the property of poorer neighbors. It was not altogether by accident that sly old Annas, father-in-law to the reigning high priest, Caiaphas, could afford the most beautiful of palaces, in which the ugliest crime in human history, the murder of the Son of God, was planned and legally justified (John 18:13 ff. and parallels).

VILLAGES, TOWNS, AND CITIES

Haphazard Grouping of Homes. — By preference the farmers and shepherds of Palestine always lived in villages rather than out by themselves on their own tracts of land. This was done partly for mutual protection from a common enemy, but largely because of the extreme sociability of the people themselves and their reluctance to be left alone. In the morning the villagers went out to work in the fields and in the evening they came home again (Ps. 104:23), except in harvest time, when they sometimes slept by the threshing floor or vineyard where they had been working (Ruth 3:1-4).

The villages seem never to have been planned, but just to have grown from generation to generation along a roadway or in the neighborhood of a convenient spring or well. Though space was practically unlimited, the houses huddled together along the hillside or in the valley, giving no evidence of group landscaping or street planning. As the village grew into a town, the crowding, and the need for straight streets and planned building, became more and more evident.

An Oriental street

Streets and Lanes. — The streets were narrow and usually crooked, probably following an old trail along which the original houses had been built. Some of the streets were so narrow and winding that they were really lanes or narrow alleys (Luke 14:21). In the smaller towns and villages and in the poorer, unpaved sections of the cities they became extremely dusty in dry weather and intolerably muddy in the rainy season. Here and there they appeared like canyons, where the bare walls of tall houses stood like cliffs on either side or where overhanging balconies almost met across the narrow space. At times they actually became tunnels beneath the second stories of the buildings which extended over them.

New Towns upon the Old. — Though the houses were originally built with their floors a little above the street level, the inhabitants regularly threw out their refuse, such as broken pottery, sweepings from the houses and roofs, as well as garbage and bones, to be picked through by the hungry dogs of the streets. Though this debris was tramped to pieces by the passersby and much of its was washed away by the rain or blown away as dust, the level of the streets gradually rose until it was above the average floor level, and steps had to be built to lead down into the homes. By this time, however, if the house was of mud brick, it probably needed to be repaired or even rebuilt. Perhaps the roof beams or bonding materials had rotted and needed to be replaced. The owner might even level the walls to the ground so that he could begin building operations anew on the old site, by this time filled in to a few feet above the street level by means of the debris and refuse of the wrecking process. Thus not only by the wanton destruction of their enemies, but also by the tearing down and rebuilding done by the inhabitants themselves, the level of ancient communities tended to become higher and higher. Some excavated communities consist of half a dozen or more separate layers of "cities," each of which contains broken pottery, utensils, and other relics. With the help of these the archaeologist determines the period of history in which the various layers of the city were built.

Walls, towers, and gates

Walls and Gates. — Many of the Palestinian towns were walled about with stone to a height sufficient to keep out the enemy. Some of the walls of very ancient times were built of huge boulders, laid up at random, not joined together with mortar, but held in position by their own weight. Such might have been the walls of ancient Jericho and the other strong fortresses of the Canaanites (Josh. 6). Other cities, especially since the time of David, were well-built masonry forts, which an enemy could take only by a long process of starvation.

In these strong walls were a number of large openings or gates, through which the traffic of the main highways entered the city. The gates were closed at sunset and opened again at sunrise (Neh. 13:19). At either side of the gate, or directly above it, strong towers, with narrow slits of windows for the use of the watchmen, guarded the approaches to the city (2 Sam. 18:24-25). At the gate of the city, where he had been awaiting news, David mourned for his son Absalom (2 Sam. 18:33). The gates themselves were heavy wooden doors, studded with strong iron nailheads, or covered with metal for extra strength. In Jerusalem the gates had various names associated with them because of the market places within (Sheep Gate, Fish Gate, Neh. 3:1, 3). Sometimes there was a small door within the large one, just large enough for a man to crawl through after the large gates had been closed. (Note: There appears to be no real evidence to support the theory that Jesus refers to this gate as the "eye of a needle" in Mark 10:25.)

Market Places. — Though in all of the streets of the villages the inhabitants might buy and sell, the businesses and trades of the larger cities tended to group themselves in certain streets and in special market places (Acts 18:3; Jer. 37:21). To these market places came the sheep and calves and goats of the shepherd, the vegetables and fruits from the farms, the fish from the Sea of Galilee and the Mediterranean. Here, too, came the traveling merchants with their shiny brass utensils, the dyers with their bright wares, the money-changers and tax collectors, the beggars and pickpockets, to ply their trade; the citizens to buy and to "window-shop" and to meet friends. Here was a cross section of the life of the community. It was a scene of noise and bustle and excitement, where wide-eyed children and curious strangers found something ever new and fascinating.

REVIEW QUESTIONS AND EXERCISES

1. a) Briefly describe the caves, booths, and mud huts used in Bible times.
   b) Describe the Bedouin tent and its furnishings.
2. How did the people of Bible times construct their houses? Include a description of
     a) the materials used in building
     b) the preparation of the foundations and the building of walls
     c) the doors and windows
     d) the materials and construction of the roof

3. In which ways did the builders provide additional rooms in the house?
4. Enumerate the chief items of furniture and equipment found in the smaller home, and show how all available space was utilized for storage purposes.
5. Draw diagrams to show the construction of various types of larger houses which included a courtyard. On the basis of this structural information try to picture the setting of the various episodes of Jesus' trial and of Peter's denial in the palace of the high priest.
6. Describe a country village with its houses, streets, and the occupations of its inhabitants.
7. Describe the gradual rebuilding of a Palestinian town upon an old site.
8. Give a brief description of the walls and gates, the streets and market places, of a fair-sized town.

PROBLEMS FOR FURTHER STUDY

1. With the help of a concordance, check the use of caves by Biblical characters, and read up on the events which brought the cave in the story.
2. Find as many examples as you can of the variety of uses to which the roof of a Palestinian home was put. As far as possible, associate each use with a significant Bible story.
3. With the help of the maps in the *Concordia Teacher's Bible* or in a Bible dictionary, study the layout of Jerusalem at the time of Christ, locating such places as the Temple, the Fortress of Antonia, the Garden of Gethsemane, the Brook Kedron, the gates and market places.

CHAPTER VI

Trades Carried On in Home and Shop

In the Romanized cities of the Near East at the time of Jesus and St. Paul, the tradesmen had united to form guilds, or unions, with well-defined laws, duties, rights and privileges for the members. Such trades tended to perpetuate themselves in families, the son naturally following the trade of his father and of his grandfather before him. People following the same trade generally lived on certain streets or in certain areas of the city. In this way they remained in close association with each other and might at times band themselves together into pressure groups to protect their source of income, as happened in the case of Demetrius, the silversmith (Acts 19:24-41).

So it had been, too, in ancient Babylonia and Egypt. Here numerous tools used by tradesmen of a by-gone age have been found, after being buried in the dry sand for 2,000 or 3,000 years or more. During the past two or three generations many have been dug up and removed to our larger museums, where they may be seen in a good state of preservation. Besides these actual remains we have scenes from the various trades painted on the walls of ancient buildings or preserved in model form in the graves of great noblemen. The ancient relics, pictures, and wooden and clay models of animals and men, and of the tools they used, combined with the information in the Scriptures and in ancient literature generally, give us a rather complete impression of the shops, tools, and handiwork of the ancient craftsmen. Travelers in the East have found modern parallels to ancient descriptions, and these help considerably in picturing the work of the tradesmen in Bible times.

In Palestine, on the other hand, a trade was usually carried on right in the house of the villager, who might at the same time be a farmer and a shepherd. He and his fellow citizens, as a group, made most of their own tools and implements, spun their own wool, wove their own cloth, molded and baked their own pottery, and tanned their own leather. All of these trades might well be represented in a fair-sized village, each by a particular family who made a specialty of it for sale or barter to the people of the community and neighborhood in general. The carrying on of a trade took up comparatively little space, since it involved mostly handwork. It could, therefore, be done right in the living room itself, or in an adjoining shop, or even under an awning stretched over the doorway and along the wide front of the house.

THE WEAVING TRADE

The Weaving of Mats. — A number of different processes were used for the weaving of mats, and the ancient remains show that the patterns, materials, and handiwork were very much like those of primitive civilizations today. In one process, strands of straw were braided together into a very long rope, which was then wound up in a close spiral and sewed into place with fiber until it had reached the desired diameter. By starting with a long line at the center, instead of beginning with a spiral, the mats could easily be woven oblong in shape. Other mats were made by laying straw or fine pliable rushes in small handfuls on the floor and weaving other strands of the same material over and under and over and under the first strands from side to side. The edges then needed to be bound with straw to keep them

Braided-mat
construction

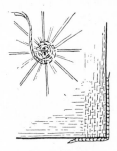

Spiral and square
weaving of mats

from fraying. Another mat had as its basic structure a dozen or so pieces of fiber, laid crossing each other at the center and radiating uniformly in all directions. Starting at the center, the weaver used a long piece of fiber, working over and under and over and under the ribs in ever-widening circles until the mat had reached the desired size. He then whipped the edges over and bound them all around to keep them from unraveling. By using straw or rush fiber, dyed in various bright colors alternating with the natural material, the weaver could obtain a great variety of patterns and color schemes.

The Weaving of Baskets. — The worker made soft, pliable baskets, similar to shopping bags, by the same method as that used in mat weaving, except that he pulled the material a little tighter each time he completed a circle so as to gradually form the basket into a hollow shape. He then wove or braided handles of the same material, working them through holes left below the rim of the basket on opposite sides. Baskets intended to be strong and rigid had to be made out of willow, dogwood, or some other tree or shrub which grew long, thin, pliable branches. Woven while the branches were fresh and green, either with or without the bark, these baskets dried into very strong and durable containers. Protective coverings with handles were woven around pottery jars used for transporting liquids. Baskets

Basket weaving

Ancient baskets

of all shapes and sizes found many uses about the home, farm, and vineyard, largely taking the place of sacks, cartons, boxes, and other containers that we use today.

Spinning. — When the freshly shorn wool came from the shepherd's flock, it needed to be carefully washed and combed, or carded, in order to straighten out the fine hairs and to remove all snags and tangles. Then the spinner took a little tuft of wool and, beginning at one end, twisted it into yarn between her fingers. As she twisted, she pulled in other strands of hair, gradually, so that the yarn remained of uniform thickness and strength as she went along. She could accomplish her purpose somewhat more rapidly and uniformly by the use of a distaff, which held a large handful of unspun wool. She gradually drew it out into a strand of the required thickness, meanwhile letting the distaff hang from the twisted yarn and keeping it spinning freely. The ancient world had no device like the mechanical spinning wheels of Colonial days.

Though cultivation of cotton and flax centered in ancient Egypt, Palestine grew great quantities of each. Flax will thrive almost anywhere, very much like the annual grasses and grains. From a small flat lozenge-shaped shiny brown seed, it grows a tall straight stem, ending in several tufts of seed heads and leaves. When the seed is fully formed, but not quite ripe, the flax is pulled up by the roots by the handful and bound into sheaves. These sheaves may be left

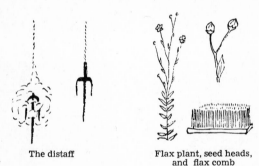

The distaff   Flax plant, seed heads,
                                   and flax comb

in the fields or taken to the housetops to dry in the sun. It was under such bundles of flax that Rahab hid the spies of Joshua (Josh. 2:6). Then the seeds are threshed out with a flail or stick, to be used as food for men and animals or to be ground and pressed for the linseed oil which they contain. To loosen the fiber from the pith and bark of the flax stem, the worker soaked the bundles of flax thoroughly for several hours or overnight. Then, handful by handful, he stripped them through the steel teeth of a brushlike flax comb until the waste fell away and a thin strand of tough fibers remained in his hand. These fibers he spun into linen thread.

Cotton, or byssus, grows in two forms in the Near East, on trees and on bushes. When ready to be used, its seed heads burst open, revealing tufts of beautiful white cotton fiber, which is then combed and spun very much like the wool described above. For cotton, as well as for linen, a smaller distaff is needed in order to produce the finer threads.

The Weaving of Cloth. — The wool, cotton, or linen threads may be made into cloth by the use of two instruments, the loom and the shuttle.

The loom is a framework of wooden slats or thin poles. Rectangular in shape, it can either be set upright in a base so that the weavers can work at it from both sides or made to rest horizontally on legs that hold it up at the desired

Looms for weaving cloth   Wooden shuttles

height above the floor. Around the edges of the framework small nails or toothpicklike wooden pegs protrude from the frame. Beginning at one edge of the frame, the weaver ties the yarn to a peg, then passes it back and forth across the frame to corresponding pegs on either side until the whole framework is covered with parallel closely set strands of yarn. If the color of the pattern is to be varied, there may be an inch or two of one color, then of another, and so on.

Now the shuttle comes into play. It is a small wooden or bone instrument, consisting of two smooth flat pointed pieces fastened together by a peg as illustrated. On the connecting peg the weaver winds the yarn which is to be used for the cross weaving. She now pushes the shuttle through between the stretched strands of yarn, above and below, alternating across the full width of the loom, returning in the same way, and thus going back and forth. Here, too, she may vary the pattern by alternately using shuttles wound with different colors of yarn.

Dyeing and Bleaching. — The people of Palestine have always loved contrasting colors, black and white, purple and yellow and red in patterns of checks and stripes. As a result of the love for color in clothing, the ancient dyer did a good business. He might make some of his own dyes from the bark of trees or roots or herbs. More likely he would import it from the East or from the great dyeworks of the Phoenician coast. Tyrian purple, made of small shellfish from the Mediterranean, ranked as the best dye of the ancient world.

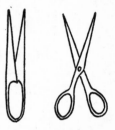
Shears and scissors

To get the desired brilliance in white cloth, the fuller soaked the thread or yarn or the finished material in a vat of clean clay paste, or "fuller's earth." He then stretched it out in the hot sun to bleach. When the material had dried, he washed it thoroughly in clear water and dried it again, ready for use. At the transfiguration of Jesus His raiment became shining, "exceeding white as snow, so as no fuller on earth can white them" (Mark 9:3).

THE CARPENTER

Jesus, the Carpenter's Son. — The trade of the carpenter will always hold some fascination for the Christian teacher because Jesus was a carpenter's Son (Matt. 13:55). No doubt He spent at least His early years working in an ordinary carpenter shop (Mark 6:3). At this trade He may have supported His mother after the death of Joseph.

The Carpenter's Shop and Its Equipment. — Though archaeologists have not found an ancient carpenter shop intact, many individual tools of various periods have been

unearthed.   These, together with the pictures of shops and
tools from ancient Egypt and Babylonia, compared with
those now in use in the Near East, give us some idea of
what a carpenter shop and its equipment looked like.

The carpenter needed a space in which he could carry
on his trade.   This might be in a room of his house or in
the street under an awning.   In his shop he placed a bench,
made of heavy planks, on which to do his work.   He also
found several wooden trestles useful for handling and sawing long material.   The ancient Egyptian monuments show
a sawing post set into the earthen floor of the shop.   To this

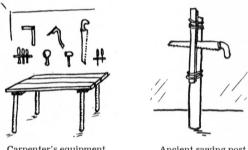

Carpenter's equipment   Ancient sawing post

post the carpenter tied the beam which he wished to rip
lengthwise.   He then stood upright as he sawed, instead
of stooping over a trestle as we do.

Tools of the Carpenter. — The carpenter's saw (Is. 10:15),
a thin blade of bronze or iron, had teeth cut into one edge.
Whether or not these teeth were set by bending one tooth
in one direction, the next in the opposite direction, the
third in the first direction and so on, so that the saw would
not bind in the wood, has not been established.   Some saws
that have been discovered are thicker at the cutting edge
than at the upper edge, thus making a wider cut than the
thinner part of the blade would need and eliminating binding.   The handle of the saw was of wood, into which the
blade was inserted and then riveted into place.

Carpenters used two similar chopping tools, the ax (Jer.

10:3) and the adze, for smoothing off wood. They also had chisels of iron or bronze, either with or without wooden handles. Hammers of iron in various shapes were fitted with wooden handles, similar to those of today. The carpenter used these to drive nails of iron as he does today (Jer. 10:4). Mallets, made of a knotty piece of wood, or other wooden hammers were used with the chisel in chipping out holes or grooves in the wood. The rough-sawed or adzed surface of the wood could also be smoothed with the chisel or with a straight square block of limestone, rubbed back and forth across the surface. It

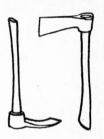

Adze and ax

may be that even a metal-bladed plane came into use in Palestine by the time of Jesus, since such instruments were in use among the Romans by about this time. The awl was useful for making small holes in the wood for starting the drill point, and for scratching marks on the wood (Ex. 21:6). The carpenter's drill worked very much like an Indian fire bow. It consisted of a bow of wood, about two feet long, with a bowstring which was wound once around a shaft

Hammer, chisel, mallet, awl, smoothing block, and cubit measure

of wood into which the drill point was fixed. In using the instrument, the carpenter set the point in the desired place, held the shaft upright under pressure of a block of wood held in his left hand, and worked the bow back and forth with his right hand, thus spinning the shaft with its sharp drill point. Drill points were interchangeable according to the size of the holes to be drilled. The process v̄as slow and tedious, but the re-

Bow drill, drill bits, chalkline, and plummet

mains of woodwork produced in ancient times show that it was effective.

In order to make straight lines for his work, the carpenter stretched a chalkline over the surface to be cut and then snapped it sharply to make a chalk mark on the wood. This method is still used by carpenters and stonecutters today. He wound the chalk line on a reel from which he could readily unwind it when he needed it again. The plumb bob, or plummet, whereby he could determine a line perpendicular to the earth, was as useful to the ancient carpenter as it is to our builders of today (Amos 7:7-8; Zech. 4:10). For marking short lines, as well as for measuring, he had his rules of wood in various lengths, marked off in fingers, or digits, palms, spans, half cubits, and cubits. (See Chapter VII, Measurements.)

Products of the Carpenter's Shop. — The carpenter of Jesus' day was not primarily a house builder, as he is today, but rather a maker of plows and yokes and other agricultural machinery, of ladders and doorways and doors and latticework for the house, and of furniture and wooden utensils useful in the home. Owing to the scarcity of good timber, the Palestinian carpenter was severely handicapped in competition with his fellow tradesmen in other countries where good wood was plentiful. When David built his grand palace, and when Solomon built the Temple, it was natural that carpenters skilled in fine woodworking had to be brought in from heavily timbered Phoenicia, where the carpenter's trade had reached its highest perfection (2 Sam. 5:11; 1 Kings 5:2-18).

Wood Carving. — Some of the carpenters became very efficient in the use of tools, particularly of knives and carving chisels. The fine goldwork in the Temple and in other elaborate buildings of the period of the kingdom usually had a finely carved wooden base over which the thin sheets of gold were hammered into place, thus giving the appearance of solid gold.

In the trade of the carpenter and wood carver there seems to have been a great deal of overlapping, according to the necessity of making a living at whatever work was to be found.

THE POTTER AND BRICKMAKER

Importance of the Industry and Source of Materials. — Attention has been called to the importance of pottery in the home. At all ages in history the potter's trade has flourished in Palestine, since there has always been a good supply of clay and a reliable domestic market for the finished product. Every housewife needed large jugs for carrying water from the spring (Gen. 24:14 f.; Eccl. 12:6) and for numerous storage purposes in the home (1 Kings 17:12). Many of her bowls, cups, and other dishes were made of pottery, which was quite fragile and often had to be replaced. Since they were so cheap, even the poor could afford to buy them (Lev. 6:28; 11:33).

In a place where there was a good clay deposit, the potter shoveled off an area of topsoil down to the layer of pure clay. Then he dug a little depression into the clay itself, filled it with water, and tramped in it with his bare feet to reduce it to the consistency of mud. He now shoveled it from the depression, as fast as it was mixed, to a pile where the water could drain off. In baskets on the back of a donkey or in a cart drawn by donkeys or oxen, he took it to his near-by pottery, where he left it on a heap outside to cure until he needed it for his trade. The place where potter's clay was dug was called a "potter's field." As the last of the clay was gradually removed, the resulting pit came to be used as the village dump. Here the people threw their broken pottery, stones from the fields, and refuse from the houses, including broken dishes and other useless articles. A waste place no longer useful for agriculture or for any other purpose, it finally was fit only as a burial ground for the poor and for unknown strangers. Thus we find the Jewish leaders buying a potter's field with the money which Judas had earned by betraying Jesus (Matt. 27:3-7).

How Pottery Was Formed. — Pottery may be roughly shaped by hand from puttylike clay, without the aid of any mechanical device, as many primitive nations still make it. Some of the ancient Palestinian pottery was made in this way. Very early, however, the invention of various types

of the potter's wheel sped up and greatly improved the process.

A very simple potter's wheel consisted of an upright shaft of wood set in a socket of stone fixed in the floor so that it could rotate easily. On the top of the shaft was fastened a "wheel" very similar to the seat of a revolving piano stool. In its simplest form the potter twirled the wheel with one hand or with the sole of his foot, while sitting cross-legged on the floor in front of it.

Hand-shaped and
wheel-molded pottery

In a more developed form the same principle is used but with a longer shaft, near the bottom of which another larger and heavier wheel is mounted. The axle, with its upper and lower wheel, is then built into a worktable so that the upper wheel is just above the level of the table. Thus the operator is able to sit on a bench next to the worktable and rest his weight on one foot while

Simple potter's wheel

keeping the wheel in motion with the other. Palestinian potters use this type of wheel today, and their forefathers may well have used it two or three thousand years ago.

Whatever the type of wheel, the operator kneads the lump of clay to puttylike consistency and then flattens it out on the wheel somewhat like a very thick pancake. He then rotates his wheel, forming the clay with his hands with

Potter's table with
wheel built in

an outward-upward pressure as it spins, until he has shaped
the bottom and the beginnings of the side wall as he wants
them. By this time his clay supply may be exhausted, so
he stops the wheel and adds another lump. This time he
arranges it in the form of a snake and lays it along the
upper rim of the partly formed pot. Rotating the wheel
again, he rubs and pushes and forms the clay to the desired
shape and thickness. He may have to add more clay in the
same way from time to time until the pot is completed. As
the clay tends to dry out in the air and to become sticky,
and finally brittle, the potter dips his hands in a dish of
water conveniently placed on his worktable and thus keeps
the material at the proper consistency for modeling. If he
should make a mistake or accidentally crack or bend or
mar the half-finished piece of work, he crushes the whole
together in his hands, mixes it with a little water, and starts
over from the beginning.

Holy Scripture refers to the potter and his clay to illustrate the relation of God to His people, "Then I went down
to the potter's house, and, behold, he wrought a work on
the wheels. And the vessel that he made of clay was marred
in the hand of the potter; so he made it again another vessel,
as seemed good to the potter to make it. Then the word of
the Lord came to me, saying, O house of Israel, cannot I do
with you as this potter? saith the Lord. Behold, as the clay
is in the potter's hand, so are ye in Mine hand, O house of
Israel" (Jer. 18:3-6). Isaiah confesses: "But now, O Lord,
we are the clay, and Thou our Potter; and we all are the
work of Thy hand" (Is. 64:8). St. Paul uses the same picture when he says, "O man, who art thou that repliest
against God? Shall the thing formed say to him that
formed it, Why hast thou made me thus? Hath not the
potter power over the clay of the same lump, to make one
vessel unto honor and another unto dishonor?" (Rom.
9:20-21).

When finished with the piece of pottery, the potter carefully sets it on a shelf, out of the wind and the sun, where

it can dry uniformly and not too rapidly for several days so that it will not crack nor check.

Baking the Pottery. — After he has accumulated quite a number of finished pieces, the potter is ready to bake, or "fire," them in a kiln of brick or stone which he has built for that purpose. Here the light pinkish-gray pieces are set up carefully in circular rows, tier above tier, so that the heat can get at them uniformly on all sides. Then the potter makes a small fire in the oven, gradually adding fuel to it until it becomes very hot. Thus the new pottery is baked so strongly that the clay becomes fused or melted together,

Small pottery kiln

with a texture about like that of our ordinary cheap red flowerpots. Then gradually the fire is permitted to die down and go out, and the kiln cools off gradually for a day or more. When it has completely cooled, the potter carefully removes the contents. For many purposes this once-fired pottery is completely satisfactory. It may be used for the storing of grain and other foodstuffs, for raisins or dates or figs.

The Glazing Process; Fine Pottery. — If the pots are intended as containers for water or particularly for the storage of precious liquids, they must go through another process called glazing. A very thin, creamy solution of an especially fine clay containing silica, or glass, is prepared. Now the pottery is either dipped into it or flushed or painted with it. This process deposits a thin but tough coating of clay, which, when baked in a very hot fire, melts and runs to a glossy-smooth finish. By using colored pigment in the clay mixture any desired color may be obtained in the glazing. A pattern may also be painted on over the flush coat before the firing process, and this design, too, will be fused into the glazed finish.

Finely formed and delicately worked earthenware has always been the pride of the potter. Though drawings and photographs give us a general idea of the art, in order to appreciate the painstaking effort, the clever handiwork, and the artistic touch of the ancient potter, one must examine the collections in a museum and then try his own hand at making it.

Brickmaking. — Though related to the work of the potter

Pottery shapes

and often performed by him, the art of making bricks was not nearly so complicated as that of making pottery. Damp clay prepared in the potter's field was tightly packed into molds the size of the brick desired. Topless and bottomless, the mold was made of four thin wooden boards with a handle projecting from one or two of them. As the clay dried, it shrank slightly so that the form could be removed easily. The bricks were then permitted to dry in the sun. Next, the workman piled them up in tiers, allowing a little air space between each two bricks. A fire built within the hollow brick structure burned them in the same way as the pottery described above. Glazed bricks were produced by coating the once-fired brick either on one side or all around with fine clay glazing material and then burning it in a very intense heat. Colored glaze resulted from the addition of pigment to the finish before the second baking. In the common bricks, particularly those which were merely baked in the sun, chopped straw was often used as bonding material to make the bricks more durable (Ex. 5:7).

THE METALWORKER

Varieties and Sources of Metals Used. — Though God had promised His people "a land whose stones are iron and out of whose hills thou mayest dig brass" (Deut. 8:9), Israel did not succeed in conquering and holding much of the mining country. She was always poor in the

Brick mold and brick

production of metal. Except when her boundaries were extended far to the north, or when her kings were strong enough to demand quantities of metal as tribute, she had to import most of her metal from other countries. Her wheat and oil and wine were traded to Tarshish in Spain in return for silver, iron, tin, and lead (Ezek. 27:12). Metal played a much larger part in ancient Palestinian life than people generally suppose. The chief metals used were the following: iron, copper, lead, zinc, tin, silver, and gold.

Iron in various compounds occurs in the mountains of Syria in workable quantities. Palestine proper has no large

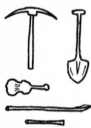

iron deposits. Copper, sometimes found in an almost pure state in the mines, is the easiest of the materials to work. Though very tough, it is soft and is therefore often combined with tin to form the alloy bronze or with zinc to form brass. Both these alloys are much harder than the copper itself and nearly as tough. Lead is found in considerable deposits in the Peninsula of Sinai. Gold was obtained from Sheba and Ophir (1 Kings 10:2; 1 Kings 22:48.)

Miner's tools: pick-
ax, shovel, mallet,
bar, and chisel

The Smelting Process. — The ancient mining country was also the heavily forested mountain region. Here the miner dug the metal ore out of the hills with pickax and crowbar and shovel, since there were no explosives and mechanical drills and air hammers as we have today. The ore was taken in carts or on the backs of donkeys to the smelter, a stone or firebrick furnace so arranged that the ore could be mixed with charcoal and the whole contents of the furnace brought to a white heat. At this stage the metal ran out from the rock and charcoal and congealed in forms provided for that purpose. Thus gold or silver, tried in the fire, lost the baser materials, the rock, the dross, and dust, with which it had been mixed, and became fine gold or fine silver (Prov. 25:4; Mal. 3:3).

Metal Casting. — The well-equipped metalworker's shop contained a small smelter in which the rough chunks of iron or copper or bits of scrap metal could be melted down in a charcoal flame brought to a white heat by a blast of air from a bellows (Jer. 6:29). An Egyptian monument shows such a bellows arrangement, consisting of two accordion-like air chambers made of wood and goatskin leather, operated by the feet of a man standing upon them, alternately stretching and compressing the bellows by raising and lowering his feet in tramping motion. The air, prevented by an arrangement of simple valves from flowing back into the bellows at each upward stroke, blasted instead

Forge, bellows, and crucibles

through a pipe in the bottom of the smelter pit. The metal became red-hot, then white-hot. Finally it began to run like sirup. The workman caught it in a fire-clay ladle and poured it into molds of the same material, where it hardened in the desired shape.

Clay molds for metal

Metal Forging. — Let us suppose that the object just cast in one of the molds is an iron axhead. It is not yet in its finished form, but rough and somewhat blunt. The metalworker lights up his forge, a smaller furnace similar to the smelter. When the charcoal is hot, he places the newly cast axhead into the hottest coals until it glows with a white heat. Then he grips it with a pair of iron tongs and takes it quickly to the anvil, a heavy block of iron or of hard stone. With a hammer he now beats it into the exact shape he wants, at the

Metalworker's tools: hammers, chisel, and tongs

same time sharpening the cutting edge by hammering it out to a knifelike thinness. He may have to reheat it several times during the process in order to make a good job. When he is finished, he allows it to cool or tempers it by dropping it into a pot of cold water. All that now remains to be done is to sharpen the edge by rubbing it on a hard stone and to fit a wooden handle into the head.

Thus each individual bronze or iron tool, sword, or spearhead was made by hand from the time of Tubalcain (Gen. 4:22) all through Bible times and almost to our own day. During the last years of the period of the Judges,

Making a bowl out of a copper sheet

Israel was so thoroughly subjugated by her enemies that no blacksmith shop was permitted to operate, not even for the purpose of repairing and sharpening agricultural implements, and the people had to be satisfied to sharpen their implements with files (1 Sam. 13:9-21).

Sheet-Metal Working. — Just as in our own day, much of the copper required in Palestine was used in the form of thin sheets, which were worked up into various utensils called "vessels of brass" in the Old Testament (Ex. 27:3; 2 Sam. 8:10; 2 Chron. 4:16). Cast into sheets as thin as possible, the metal was beaten or rolled to uniform thickness, then cut into the desired shape for hammering.

Let us suppose that a wash-basin-shaped copper bowl is to be made. The workman cuts out a circle of sheet copper, holds it by the outer rim between his thumb and forefinger, and lets the center of it rest on his anvil or on a piece of very hard wood or lead. Then with a round-headed hammer he lightly and rapidly taps it, as he gradually rotates it so that the hammer taps move in a gradually widening spiral towards the outer rim. He repeats this process over and over. Soon the sheet becomes slightly concave, and then more and more so until the metal has been stretched to the required depth and shape. He now hammers a rim around the edge, makes up the required handles out of the same metal, and rivets them in place. Then he polishes the finished product with sand or rock dust until it glistens in the light.

Not only basins, but cups and bowls, pitchers and plates, ladles and spoons, were hammered out of sheet metal. Knives, saws, sickles, and other tools and implements were also products of the metalworker's shop. Ancient Damascus, capital of Syria, developed metalworking to a high degree of perfection, as did also the Babylonians, Egyptians, and the Israelites themselves.

The Gold- and Silversmith. — In a very refined way the processes described above were also used in the production of utensils and jewelry of the precious metals, gold and silver. The smelters, hammers, tongs, and chisels or "graving tools" and anvils were smaller. The metals themselves were easier to work without heating. Thus the gold- or silversmith was able to produce work of the finest quality out of these precious metals (Is. 40:19; Is. 41:7; Acts 19:24). While silver tarnishes easily and eventually disintegrates through oxidation, gold retains its brilliance much longer. The craftsmen who wrought the fine work of gold and silver and brass in the Temple devoted their best artistic efforts to the service of God (1 Kings 7:13-51).

THE TANNER AND LEATHERWORKER: OTHER TRADES

Location and Equipment of Tanneries. — It is not at all by accident that the house of Simon, the tanner with whom Peter lodged in Joppa, was by the seaside (Acts 10:6). There were at least three reasons for this, namely, the need for a plentiful supply of water and for facilities to drain off used chemical refuse. Then there was the social pressure which forced such an offensive trade away from the better residential neighborhoods to the already smelly waterfront. The tanner needed a house or a shop for the storage of his hides as well as for the large vats and tanks in which he cured the leather.

Curing and Tanning the Hides. — As the hides came from the slaughterer, they still had the hair of the animal on one side and a layer of fatty tissue and dried blood on the other. All loose matter was first scraped off by laying the hide over a log set in the sandy beach or in the floor of the shop at an angle of about 30 degrees. In this

Tanner's log, scraper, and vat

scraping process the craftsman used a curved instrument, somewhat like a modern carpenter's drawknife, with which he scraped the hide on the flesh side. Next he soaked it in a vat containing a solution of lime or lye, which loosened the hair and the fatty matter still remaining. Putting it back on his log once more, he scraped it again until it was clean and soft. After carefully rinsing it in clean water, he immersed it in a tanning solution. We do not know the exact formula of the ancient tanning compounds, but no doubt they were made of the bark of certain types of oak trees which are still used to cure the rawhide into leather. If soft leather was desired, the worker rubbed the skin with animal oil, similar to our neat's-foot product, and kneaded and scraped it until it was thoroughly dry. Depending on the purpose for which it was to be used, leather could be dyed any color or given any desired finish.

Leatherworker's tools: awls, needles, knives, and bench

Leatherworking Tools and Leather Goods. — The tanner himself might be a leatherworker, or he might sell his product to one who made a specialty of this highly developed craft. The leatherworker needed a low bench, similar to that of the cobbler of a generation or two ago. He had various types and sizes of awls, sharp naillike pieces of metal held in a wooden handle. He used knives of several shapes to cut his leather, and needles and waxed linen thread to sew it up into the various articles. He also had tools to press patterns into the leather, like those which leather craftsmen use today. He worked up heavy cowhide into soles of sandals, various parts of soldier's armor, aprons for workmen, belts, etc. He used the finer types of leather for shoes and purses for the wealthy (Ezek. 16:10). Fine ram skins dyed red, as well as badger skins (R. V., sealskins), were used extensively in the construction of the Tabernacle (Ex. 25:5).

Tentmaking. — Tentmaking is of interest to us because St. Paul learned it in his youth and followed it at various times during his missionary career (Acts 18:3). In the nomadic East, tents of all kinds found a ready market. On account of the extreme glare of the sun, which the Easterner shunned even more than our own grandparents did, the owners fitted their houses with awnings of all kinds to keep the interior in semidarkness, while at the same time providing porch space in the street. Tents of all shapes described in Chapter V were the product of the tentmaker.

Tools of the stonecutter: hammer, mallet, chisel, and saw

Tentmakers made the fabric for their best tents of goats' hair (Ex. 25:4). Others were made of cotton or of coarser fibers. The tools used were knives and shears, awl, and needle and thread, very similar to those of the leatherworker.

Stonecutting. — In Palestine, richly blessed with good limestone, the stonecutter's art flourished, particularly in the time of David and Solomon and up to the captivity, and again under Roman influence, at the time of the Herods, when great building projects sprang up.

The ancient stonecutter took great blocks of stone from the quarries by the use of pickaxes and crowbars, supplemented by chisels and mallets and hammers and saws and drills, similar to those used by the carpenter. Newly exposed limestone can be cut with a saw almost as easily as ice.

A drill point of iron or flint readily ground its way into the rock. In order to split off a large slab of rock, the worker drilled a row of holes to a depth of about six inches. He then inserted a wedge of wood into each hole and tapped each wedge lightly with a hammer, over and over again in rotation all along the row, until the desired stone block split off clean. Sometimes he forced pegs tightly into the holes and then kept them soaked with water until the expansion of the water-soaked wood split off the rock. By the use of an iron chisel and mallet, or a stonecutter's hammer,

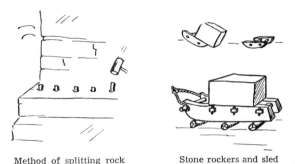

Method of splitting rock   Stone rockers and sled
on rollers

he then dressed the stone down to the desired shape and smoothness.

The stonecutter made sills and lintels for doors and windows, paving blocks for fine buildings, carved stones to be used in doorway arches or as the heads of pillars and columns, great cylindrical sections of columns for the support of porches or colonnades, stone benches for formal gardens and courtyards, as well as mills and mortars and other stone implements and utensils.

The large blocks of stone were laboriously moved on low heavy-wheeled carts or on rollers, requiring the power of thousands of men and animals for jobs which can be done quickly and without effort by today's highly developed machines.

The Gem Cutter. — The ancient gem cutter, who was perhaps also a goldsmith as well as a jeweler, became adept in cutting and grinding and polishing precious and semi-precious stones of all kinds for use in bracelets, necklaces, strings of beads, pendants, and rings. He also made little flasks and boxes for cosmetics and ointments. His hammers, chisels, files, and drills were similar to those of the stonecutter, but much smaller and more carefully made.

REVIEW QUESTIONS AND EXERCISES

1. How was it possible for trades in Palestine to be carried on right in the homes of the workers? Show that the weaving of mats and baskets was especially adapted to home industry and describe the processes.
2. Outline the process of spinning wool into yarn and weaving it into cloth.
3. Describe the shop, common tools, and chief products of the carpenter.
4. Why was the potter's trade very important in the life of the Biblical community? Briefly describe the method of making pottery, from the gathering of the clay to the baking of the finished product. What is a "potter's field"?
5. Describe briefly the mining, smelting, and casting of copper or iron.
6. How were copper pots and dishes made?
7. How was leather manufactured in Bible times? List the articles of clothing and equipment which were ordinarily made of leather.
8. Describe the tools and product of the tentmaker.
9. What kind of tools did the stonecutter use? Describe how he split off great blocks of stone in the quarry.
10. With what materials did the jeweler work, and what were the products of his art?

PROBLEMS FOR FURTHER STUDY

1. As a project for yourself or your Sunday school class, look up the patterns and materials used in weaving mats and baskets as illustrated in Biblical encyclopedias or in books describing Biblical life. Try your own hand at a few samples of weaving in the various materials and patterns in order to illustrate the process to Sunday school children or to the teachers. You might also try cloth weaving, using heavy woolen yarn or wrapping cord and a small homemade rectangular wooden frame about 10×10 inches, with small headless brads driven in at $\frac{3}{16}$-inch intervals.

2. Expand the picture of God as the Potter and His people as clay in His hands. Apply the Scripture references Is. 64:8; Jer. 18:3-6 to the life of a Sunday school teacher as molded by God. What instrument does He use in this process?

3. Clay is available at any brickyard or pottery, or it may be bought at school or art-supply houses. Simple pottery is easy to make even without a wheel. You may bake it in the sun or in an ordinary oven at home. Small bowls are easiest to make. Be sure that the opening is left large. Begin with very simple vessels.

CHAPTER VII

The Arts and Sciences; Travel, Trade, and Commerce

There is a certain amount of artistry connected with each of the crafts and trades discussed in Chapter VI. The carpenter was a tradesman, yet when he worked at fine carpentry or wood carving or inlay work of wood and ivory, he became an artist in a very real sense of the word. The stonecutter might be said to have engaged in a trade, yet when he did fine stone carving, and particularly when he worked on a precious stone, his craft became an art. So it was, too, with the metalworker as he tended toward the finer work in gold and silver, and with the potter as he applied the finest material and workmanship to the development of his art.

THE ARTS

Sculpture. — Much of the art of the ancient Egyptians, Babylonians, Phoenicians, Syrians, Persians, Greeks, and Romans was devoted to the making of images, shrines, models of temples, or of other articles connected with idolatrous worship. Demetrius, the silversmith, made a business, and perhaps even a "racket," of this type of art (Acts 19: 24 f.). Knowing human failings and sinfulness, the Lord embodied in the First Commandment the direct prohibition: "Thou shalt not make unto thee any graven images, or any likeness of anything that is in heaven above or that is in the earth beneath or that is in the water under the earth. Thou shalt not bow down thyself to them, nor serve them, for I the Lord thy God am a jealous God . . ." (Ex. 20:4-5; cp. Deut. 4:16-19 and Deut. 27:15). But since God Himself revealed the specifications of the Tabernacle to Moses, and later those of the Temple to Solomon, and these specifications included artistic designs and figures of flowers, fruits, palms, oxen, and even of cherubims, it is evident that what God meant in Exodus was this, "Thou shalt not make images or likenesses of anything on the earth *in order* to bow down to them or to worship them." According to the above principle it was permissible that the brazen "sea," or large basin in the Temple should be held up by molten oxen.

But when Israel fell so low as to make golden calves *for worship,* repeating what Israel had done in Moses' absence on Mount Sinai in the wilderness (Ex. 32:1 f.), by worshiping Jeroboam's calves at Bethel and Dan (1 Kings 12:26-33), God's prophet plainly warned against the abuse and announced a curse upon Jeroboam (1 Kings 13:1 f.). Later, at Ahab's time, Israel fell even deeper into gross worship of the Baal

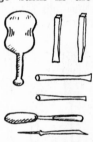

Ancient "graving" tools

images (1 Kings 16:30-33; 1 Kings 18:17-46). So also did Judah in later years, against the warnings of Isaiah, Jeremiah, and the other prophets (Is. 44:9 f.; Jer. 10:3 f.), until finally God took away His people into bondage (2 Chron. 36:17-21). In heathen Babylon, amidst idolatrous worshipers, the Jews turned from the tendency to become idolaters themselves. Upon their return to Palestine, under Ezra and Nehemiah, there was no further idol worship. Instead, the rabbis prohibited everything that might even suggest idolatry. No images of animals or angels appeared in the new Temple or in the local synagogs. Josephus, the Jewish historian, says that even in the homes of the wealthy such decoration was forbidden (Josephus, *Antiquities,* 17, 6, 2; Josephus, *Wars,* 2, 10, 4). It was this spirit which prompted the defeated

Jews not to permit their Roman conquerors to march into Jerusalem carrying the emperor's image on their standards (*Antiquities,* 18, 3, 1; *Wars,* 2, 9, 2). It was natural that under the pressure of this puritanic trend sculpture was discouraged almost to the point of extinction. Just as the bare "meeting houses" of the American Puritans reflected the Calvinistic view that the use of everything which had been devoted to idolatrous purposes by the Roman Catholics, such as crosses, crucifixes, and statues, might possibly tempt the people in the direction of idolatry, so the houses of worship of the Jewish puritans testified to the belief that such artistic productions might become a snare to the congregation and should therefore be omitted.

Egyptian paint
brushes of fiber

Painting. — Painting enjoyed a strong development in Egypt. Here the Israelites must have learned, or at least have observed, its methods and techniques, yet in Palestine itself they did not develop the art, as far as we know. Thus it happens that while we know exactly what many of the ancient Pharaohs looked like, along with hundreds of other heathen dignitaries of Old Testament times, we have no pictures or statues of Moses, or David, or Solomon, or Isaiah, or Daniel. And while we have exact knowledge of the appearance of Julius Caesar and Augustus and Tiberius and Nero, we haven't the slightest inkling of what Matthew or Luke or Paul or Jesus Himself may have looked like.

Writing and Writing Materials. — Some method of recording thought seems to be necessary for the development of ideas in the sciences. This is true to the extent that peoples who have not been able to write have never advanced very far culturally.

Job, who was probably a contemporary of Abraham, forefather of the Israelites, wished that his words might be written in a book (Job 19:23). We know that at the time of Abraham the Babylonians had already recorded their complete set of laws as well as a great many other literary works. By the time of the Exodus the art of composition was so highly developed that Moses, brought up as he was in the learning of the Egyptians, could write the history of his people and could make a record of God's directions for their faith and lives in a set of five books, which while they

Stylus and clay tablet

are *God's* Word, are yet the finest product of *man's* writing in the literature of the period. Writing must have been rather common at least among the professional classes, the judges and the priests, at the time of the Exodus (Ex. 17:14; Deut. 24:1 ff.; Num. 5:23).

The Babylonians wrote their literary works, as well as their letters and bills and receipts, on small tablets of clay into which they pressed a chisellike stylus to make the wedge-shaped characters. Then they allowed the clay to dry or even baked it to make it durable. If the message was particularly important, they covered it with another thin coating of clay, both to keep its contents secret and to protect it from rough handling. Important proclamations and other documents were chiseled into the solid rock, or on monuments or on tablets of stone, as

Parchment scroll or "book"

were the Ten Commandments which God gave to Moses (Ex. 31:18; 32:15-16).

The ordinary material which the Israelites used to write their important documents upon was parchment, the skin of goats or of sheep. Carefully scraped until it was thin and clean and almost transparent, it was then smoothed out until it became a fine-textured writing surface. In contrast to our practice the Hebrews wrote in columns from right to left. When he had finished his writing, the scribe rolled up his parchment strip into a scroll (Ps. 40:7; Jer. 36:23). The Israelites may also have used papyrus, as the Egyptians did. The Egyptians made papyrus of the inner layers of the papyrus stalk. After unrolling the layers from a length

of the stalk, they laid them flat side by side on a smooth wet surface. Then they laid another thickness on top of them at right angles and pressed the two layers together so that, when dry, they became one sheet of very strong paper.

Instead of a pencil or a pen the writer used a stylus of reed or of wood, which he dipped in black ink (Jer. 36: 18; 2 John 12). The scribe commonly

Papyrus reed and method of making paper

carried paper or parchment, his stylus, and a horn of ink at his girdle (Ezek. 9:2). For writing on metal or stone, an iron stylus served to scratch or chisel out the letters (Job 19:24; Jer. 17:1).

Literature. — Aside from the fact that the Bible is God's inspired Word, each of the Hebrew writers has left the stamp of his own style on his writings. The Old Testament consists of several types of literature. The historical books, with the laws and prophecies and doctrines woven into them, give us a connected story of God's people as well as a clear picture of their virtues, their sins, their repentance, and their hope of salvation. The poetic books, including Job, the Psalms, Proverbs, and Ecclesiastes, teach us God's will and assist us in properly worshiping Him. The prophetic books, beginning in the period of decline, point to the great events of the future and, above all, to the coming of the Savior of mankind. All of these books together form a complete literature, the like of which appears nowhere else in world history.

Scribe's stylus and inkhorn

During and after the exile the Jews produced many other religious books modeled after the Scriptures themselves. Some of these we know well as the Old Testament Apocrypha, which were often printed in the older Bibles along with the canonical books and which the Roman Catholic Church regards as part of the Holy Scriptures. Of many other books we have the titles or very brief descriptions or excerpts. In the centuries just before the coming of Jesus the Jews of the Dispersion produced an abundance of religious literature, written no longer in the Hebrew language, but in the everyday Aramaic or, like the New Testament books, in Greek, the literary language of the day.

Music and Musical Instruments. — We know very little about ancient music, not even the intervals of the scale employed. To us it would doubtless sound as strange and weird as does oriental music today. The various instruments played only the melody, in contrast to the harmonies of our modern orchestration.

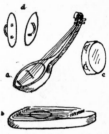

Musical instruments: (a) kinnor, (b) instrument of 10 strings, (c) tambourine (d) cymbals

The invention of musical instruments goes back to Jubal, a descendant of Cain, who "is the father of all such as handle the harp and the organ (stringed and wind instruments," Gen. 4:21). These two types, together with the percussion devices, include all the musical instruments mentioned in the Bible.

Among the *stringed instruments* the *kinnor* (1 Sam. 16: 23), translated "harp," probably similar to a guitar, was played with the fingers (1 Sam. 18:10) or with a wooden or bone plectrum. This instrument had gut strings and a stretched-skin sounding board. The musicians could even play it walking (1 Sam. 10:5; 2 Sam. 6:5). The *"instrument of ten strings"* (Ps. 33:2) consisted of a shallow oblong box.

The strings were metal wires stretched across the wooden sounding board. A great variety of harps, guitars, and lyres appears on the Egyptian monuments. Undoubtedly many of these were also used in Palestine, though it is difficult to make a positive identification in any Scripture references.

One of the most popular of the *percussion instruments,* the timbrel, or tambourine, consisted of a light wooden hoop with rawhide stretched tightly across its surface and disks of metal set into slits in the wooden rim. Women usually used it, shaking it rhythmically with one hand and tapping the rawhide surface with the fingers of the other hand, to keep time for their ceremonial dancing (Judg. 11:34, Jephthah's daughter). Cymbals, consisting of disks of brass (1 Chron. 15:19), which were clashed together, were used in the Temple service (1 Chron. 25:1, 6). The tabret, mentioned in 1 Sam. 18:6, may have been a device similar to the triangle. The sistrum was a large metal ring from which hung smaller rings and bars of metal (2 Sam. 6:5).

Wind instruments: horn and trumpet of brass, ram's-horn and cow-horn trumpets, flute and double flute

Of the *wind instruments* the pipe, or flute, made of reed, the favorite instrument of country folk, provided music for weddings or for funerals or for whiling away the time of the lonely shepherds (Matt. 9:23; Rev. 18:22; Is. 5:12). It was not used in public worship, as far as we know. The cornet, or the trumpet, developed from the curved horn of an animal, but later made of silver, had a brilliant penetrating tone. It served like our church bells to call people to worship. Instead of being bent into an elongated coil as our trumpets are, it was left in one long straight tube with a flared-out end. The horn, or trombone, with a somewhat lower pitch but a very penetrating tone, was also used at religious services. The sackbut (Dan. 3:5) was a bagpipe with a shrill, penetrating tone similar to that of the Scotch pipes.

In their rejoicing over their deliverance from Pharaoh's host, Miriam and the other women went out "with timbrels and with dances," chanting the praises of God for His mercy to them (Ex. 15:20). This was also done at the observance of the major festivals of rejoicing (1 Kings 1:40). Solemn chanting marked the periods of national or family mourning (Jer. 9:17-18; 2 Chron. 35:25; Matt. 9:23).

Girls and women danced among themselves for social pastime (Jer. 31:4). The children of the street, like our children today, were as quick to imitate their elders in dancing as in mourning (Luke 7:32; Job 21:11). Occasionally, too, we hear of men dancing under the stress of great emotion, as when David and his men danced before the Ark of the Lord (2 Sam. 6:5; 2 Sam. 6:14). The ancient dancing consisted of rhythmic steps in circular movements, accompanied by the tapping of tambourines or the rhythm of other percussion instruments. There is no trace whatever of any dancing between the sexes, nor is there any sign that female dancers indulged in the shameless motions and exposure that became all too common among the Greeks and Romans of New Testament times. When Herodias' daughter, Salome, danced before Herod, she was probably carrying out a Roman custom that fit in very well with the rest of the wantonness and debauchery of a typical Roman feast (Matt. 14:6).

THE SCIENCES

Consciousness of Nature. — There is a refreshing consciousness of nature in the Old Testament, particularly in the Psalms of David and the works of Solomon. David, the shepherd boy, alone in the mountains with his sheep, developed that same kinship with God's lowliest creatures that is shown by our Lord Himself, with His interest in the lilies of the field, the fowl of the air (Matt. 6:26-28), and the two sparrows sold for a farthing (Matt. 10: 29). Solomon, wisest of men, "spake of trees, from the cedar tree that is in Lebanon even unto the hyssop that springeth out of the wall. He spake also of beasts, and of fowl, and of creeping things, and of fishes" (1 Kings 4: 32–33). There must have been a great many treatises written by Solomon which have not come down to us. The Book of Job, too, shows a broad knowledge of nature. Yet the Bible is not a textbook of botany or zoology; it merely mentions these things in passing. The later rabbinical literature shows a considerable interest in nature, combining a strange mixture of speculation and superstition with real scientific knowledge, but science in the modern sense of the word was not practiced by the Jews.

Medicine and Healing. — Ever since the Fall the human race has been subject to illness, which is the result of sin and a foretaste of death. The Bible contains many references to sickness and to healing; yet there is not sufficient information for us to determine just how much the ancient Israelites knew about disease. No doubt they became acquainted with the medical practices of Egypt and in New Testament times with those of the Greeks and Romans. St. Luke was the beloved physician of St. Paul (Col. 4: 14) and remained with him when he was needed most (2 Tim. 4: 11).

There is not very much information concerning the extent to which internal medicine was prescribed. Certainly, at least the upper classes had the services of physicians in Old Testament times (2 Chron. 16: 12). At the time of Jesus we hear of the unfortunate woman with an issue of blood "which had spent all her living upon physicians, neither could be healed of any," as St. Luke, himself a physician, says (Luke 8: 43). St. Mark puts it much more bluntly, noting that "she had suffered many things of many physicians and had spent all that she had and was nothing bettered, but rather grew worse" (Mark 5:25-26). No doubt the common people had to rely on their own home remedies made of roots and herbs and berries, according to recipes passed down from generation to generation. As noted in Chapter III, the use of dried fruits, olive oil, and the roughage in whole wheat flour and other foods did much to eliminate the necessity for physics and purgatives which have become all too common in our modern civilization.

External medication was used very extensively. Wounds and bruises were cleansed with water or with wine, anointed with olive oil, and then bandaged (Is. 1:6; Luke 10:34). Soothing ointments and salves were prepared from various herbs. The East Jordan country was famous for the balm of Gilead, made of the sap of a tree (Jer. 8:22; 46:11). Lumps of boiled figs served as poultices for boils (2 Kings 20:7).

There still are warm medicinal springs in the vicinity of the Dead Sea, where, according to Josephus, Herod went for relief from his ailment (*Antiquities*, 16, 6, 5; *Wars*, 1, 33, 5). Sufferers from rheumatism, arthritis, or the aches and pains of malaria would find welcome relief in such springs. The first symptoms of leprosy, the most dreaded of diseases, were carefully watched. When the scaly skin, the loosening fingernails, and the falling hair had definitely established the existence of the disease, the unfortunate sufferer was removed forever from the company of other people. Physicians apparently made no effort to heal the disease, since it was considered a curse which could only be removed by a miracle of God Himself. Palsy, or paralysis, was very common and considered incurable. Acute eye infections, increased by the sun's glare and the filthy dust of the streets, often led to blindness. Most of the other diseases mentioned in the Bible have been identified, but we have little information as to the materials or methods used in their treatment. One thing we do know, they all yielded to the almighty power of Jesus, the Great Physician, as is attested by His numerous miracles of healing.

Surgeons, using instruments remarkably like our own, attempted delicate operations of all kinds, but, without the knowledge of anaesthetics and antiseptics, these could not be very successful on a major scale. We have no information as to how much the Jews practiced surgery.

It is noteworthy that while charms and amulets of various kinds are common in the Near Eastern countries of today, there is no mention whatever of such faith-healing or magic devices in the Scriptures.

Mathematics and Physics. — Moses certainly learned something of mathematics and astronomy from the Egyptians. We know that the Israelites in the wilderness knew enough of the fundamentals of arithmetic to compute their weights and measures, as well as the dimensions and distances for the construction of the tabernacle. They also understood geometry, or "earth measurement," sufficiently to measure and allot land in Palestine at the time of the conquest under Joshua. By New Testament times the physical sciences had advanced remarkably in the Greek world. No doubt St. Paul, St. Luke, and other well-educated men had a fair scientific knowledge, but the Bible itself is silent on this point, as in so many others which are not vital to its central message of sin and grace.

Architecture. — The painstaking detail necessary in the construction of the elaborate palace of David and of Solomon, and especially of the Temple, indicates that the science of architecture had also advanced among the Israelites, although Hiram's Tyrian architects, as well as artisans, may have done much of this work. At the time of Jesus and St. Paul the architecture of Jerusalem and other large Jewish cities tended to be Greek or Roman rather than Jewish. The fine sense of proportion and balance and the solid construction of the ancient Greek public buildings have never been surpassed, except perhaps in our own generation. Outstanding examples of architecture in New Testament Jerusalem were the Temple of Herod and the great palaces of the wealthy and of the priests, who spared no expense to make them as outstanding as any in the world of that day.

Astronomy. — Like all the ancient nations of the Near East the Hebrews were very conscious of the heavenly bodies. When Abraham at God's command looked to the heavens to count the stars (Gen. 15:5), they must have seemed to him so close that he could almost touch them, as they still appear in those regions today. The sun was extremely bright in the day time, and the moon was looked upon as dangerous at night (Ps. 121:6). The Hebrews recognized some of the constellations. Job mentions Arcturus, Orion, and Pleiades; and Amos speaks of "the seven stars and Orion" (Amos 5:8). However, the Hebrew calendar was not scientifically set and adjusted according to the relative positions of the stars, and it is therefore less accurate than that of Babylonia or Egypt.

TIME AND THE CALENDAR

Disregard of Time; "the Unhurried East." — Western travelers are struck by the complacent disregard of time in the Near East. The rush and bustle of the machine age, to which the western world has accustomed itself, seems foolish to an Oriental. If a task does not reach completion today, it will wait until tomorrow or next week or next year. If a father cannot complete a certain unit of work, perhaps his son can, or even his grandson. The ordinary units of time were the same among Bible peoples as they are now — the day, the week, the month, and the year.

The Day; Day and Night. — The Hebrew day began at

sunset and ended at sunset of the next day (Gen. 1:5; Lev. 23:32). Day and night averaged twelve hours each, though in the various seasons they ranged from ten to fourteen hours. In ancient times it appears that the night was divided into three watches of four hours each, (Judg. 7:19), while later the plan common to the Roman Empire provided four watches of three hours each. The sundial (2 Kings 20:11; Is. 38:8) was probably in general use among the well-to-do, and the water clock employed by neighboring peoples no doubt also served to tell time in Palestine, at least from late Old Testament times on.

The Week and Month. — The week consisted of six work-days, followed by the Sabbath, the day of rest, the sanctity of which was protected by the Mosaic laws. The changing phases of the moon determined the Hebrew month. The new moon was hailed with a sound of trumpets as the beginning of another month. It appears that at first the Hebrews numbered their months and only in later times named them. Both names and numbers appear in various places in Scripture. Beginning in spring, the months ran as follows: Nisan, Iyar, Sivan, Tammuz, Ab, Elul, Tishri, Marchesh-van, Chisleu, Tebeth, Shebat, Adar. Since our months are based on the sun, while the Hebrew months were based on the moon, they do not quite fit our reckoning, but, roughly, Nisan corresponds with April; Iyar, roughly, with May, and so forth.

The Year. — Nisan, or April, the opening of spring, began the year, according to the law of Moses (Ex. 12:2; Ex. 23:15), and the whole Old Testament cycle of religious festivals rests on this reckoning. The agricultural year, on the other hand, began in the fall (Ex. 23:16), as did the sabbatic years and the years of jubilee (Lev. 25:9-10). There are really only two seasons in Palestine, summer and winter, but special seasonal periods are the barley harvest in late spring, the wheat harvest in early summer, the harvest of grapes in midsummer, and the time of sowing in fall.

TRAVEL AND TRANSPORTATION BY LAND AND SEA

Travel in General. — From the time of Cain on, mankind has tended to migrate to find new pastures, new agricultural land, new security or new freedom (Gen. 4:16). The story of the patriarchs began with the command to Abraham, *"Get thee out* of thy country and from thy kindred and from thy father's house unto a land that I will show thee" (Gen. 12:1). A generation later Abraham's servant traveled to Mesopotamia to get a wife for Isaac. Isaac's son Jacob followed the same route to escape from his brother Esau. Traders bought Joseph from his brothers and took him along to Egypt, beginning a chain of events which led all of Israel to that country (Gen. 37:27; Gen. 46:6). For 40 years Israel traveled about in the wilderness of Sinai before each family finally received its allotment of land a generation later under Joshua. Within the Holy Land itself a considerable amount of traveling back and forth took place over the highways in connection with trade and with the periodic festivals. Jesus, like other young people, must have eagerly looked forward to the time when He would make one of these journeys for the first time (Luke 2:42).

As the roads in our own country tend to follow an older trail made by some pioneer following the line of least resistance across the country, so the old Palestinian roads wound through valleys and gorges, along mountain ridges, and across fords in the river, as they had done for hundreds of years. Travelers of today still cover about the same distances, stop at the same khans or springs or wells of water. Since roads between the more important communities carried more traffic than others, they received considerable attention, reaching the highest point of development in the Roman military highways, over which Jesus traveled. The average country road was very poorly kept, dusty in summer, and almost impassable in the rainy season.

Travel by Foot. — Bible people traveled short distances and even made very long journeys on foot. This meant that the traveler had to carry with him everything he needed on the way, his staff, his cloak for protection during the night, his scrip, or purse, with food for the journey, and his jar or dried gourd filled with water (Gen. 21:14). The scrip, or purse, made of leather, might contain dried fruit, nuts, parched wheat, and perhaps a little bread. Thus equipped, whole companies traveled together on foot to attend the festivals. They made a picnic of the journey, camping along the way or staying overnight at khans, resting several hours at noonday, and eating lunch together along the way. Women and small children might ride on donkeys (Luke 10:34).

A khan

The Inn, or Khan. — At convenient stopping places, such as the edge of the desert, the ford of a river, or an oasis or spring, the inn or khan did as good a business as filling stations and tourist homes do along the main highways today. In its simplest form the inn might be an area surrounded by a stone wall, except for one opening with a strong door. Here travelers could find security and some conveniences when they camped for the night under their own tents. A well-developed inn consisted of a courtyard into which a roof extended inward from the walls on all sides, forming a sort of shed all the way around the open court. This might be two stories high, in which case the ground floor was rented to the travelers for their animals and baggage, while the upper story was reserved for the people themselves. It has been suggested that Jesus was born in the lower story, or "stable," of such a khan, since there was no space left unoccupied in the room above, where people would normally spend the night.

Travel by Camel Caravan or Wagon Trail. — On the fringes of the desert long-distance travelers formed camel trains, a group of merchants uniting for mutual companionship and protection. During the day the camels traveled in single file, carrying their packs and at times their masters as well. Wagons, open or covered (Num. 7:3), were used more extensively in ancient times than some people imagine. The Egyptian Pharaoh sent wagons, probably drawn by chariot horses, to transport Joseph's family and their possessions to Egypt (Gen. 45:19 ff.). In Palestine itself, as well as in the countries to the east, oxen or cows normally served as draft animals (1 Sam. 6:7; 2 Sam. 6:6). Though in very early Babylonian times four-wheeled wagons appear, the people of Bible times, as well as those of the Near East of today, commonly use two-wheeled carts. Such a cart consisted of a wooden platform set on a heavy wooden axle, fitted with wooden wheels. The wheels were of solid construction, sometimes made of three or four heavy planks of wood fastened together with two crosspieces, cut into circular shape, and held together by a tire of iron or of rawhide. From the platform a tongue extended to which the yoke of the oxen was secured. (Compare Chapter II, "Yokes.") Great trains of these wagons, each

Papyrus boat
Wooden boat

drawn by one or two teams of oxen, still wind across the plains of Mesopotamia, as did our own covered wagons over the prairie trails of the West a few generations ago.

Boats, Ferries, and Rafts. — In the Egyptian delta region the Israelites had seen various types of boats, from the small raftlike craft to the palatial yachts of the wealthy. Along the Jordan and its lakes the inhabitants used small boats for fishing as well as for transportation, (John 6:22). No doubt these resembled the simple wooden boats of today, built of boards overlapped on each other and caulked with fiber and pitch to make them watertight. Sometimes favorable winds made the use of sails possible (Luke 8:23), though ordinarily the boatmen had to depend upon their oars. On the Jordan of today some boats consist of a light framework of green wood over which skin is stretched. Though these are very buoyant, they are difficult to steer or to paddle upstream. Rafts were made of inflated skins of animals covered by a platform of wood. These were as buoyant and as useful for ferrying heavy materials across rivers as our own army rafts of today. After the defeat of Absalom, David and his household returned across the Jordan on a ferryboat (2 Sam. 19:18). Quite probably there was regular ferry service across the Jordan River at several points, as well as across the Sea of Galilee, just as there is today.

Sea-Going Ships. — Encouraged by the fine harbors

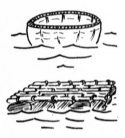

Skin boat and raft

along their rocky shores, the people of Phoenicia have always been great shipbuilders. The coastline of Palestine, however, contains few harbors of any kind and not a single good one. To the south the land allotted to Israel had remained in the hands of the Philistines. To the north even David never conquered the coastal strip of Phoenicia originally assigned to the tribe of Asher as far as the city of Sidon. Though Solomon sent out great fleets of ships to trade in the Persian Gulf and with the countries to the east in gold and silver and precious stones (1 Kings 9:26; 10:11-12), outside his reign it was very seldom that Israel carried on much foreign trade. The merchant mariners of Phoenicia were the traders of the ancient world. In the last four centuries before Christ and throughout New Testament times great fleets of ships carried the goods of Egypt, Syria, Phoenicia, and Greece to the western Mediterranean as far as Rome, Sicily, and Spain. It was on one of these ships that St. Paul suffered shipwreck. The story of the storm and wreck given by St. Luke in the Book of Acts is considered the finest description of such a tragedy in all ancient literature (Acts 27:10—28:5).

BUSINESS METHODS, MEASURES, WEIGHTS, MONEY

Business Instinct of the Jews; the Spread of Their Commerce in the Dispersion. — The Jewish people seem always to have had a strong business instinct. Their ancestor Jacob could drive a hard bargain with his brother Esau (Gen. 25:29-34). His Uncle Laban seems to have possessed even more of that shrewdness which so often fails to draw a clear distinction between a sharp business deal and outright crookedness (Gen. 29:18-28; Gen. 30:27-43).

The Lord's intention seems to have been that His people earn their living under His divine blessing by working the rich soil which He had allotted to them (Deut. 16:15). With the surplus of the products of the pasture, the farmland, and the vineyard they were to trade with foreign nations for the type of goods which they themselves could not produce.

And yet the very location of Israel was in itself a strong inducement for the development of foreign trade, strategically located as she was between the great commercial nations of antiquity: the Greek island and mainland to the northwest, Phoenicia and Syria to the north, the succession of great peoples which dominated Mesopotamia to the northeast and east, Edom and Moab and the desert people in general to the southeast and south, and Egypt to the southwest. The three main roads between these nations passed along the Mediterranean coast, over the mountains west of the Jordan River and through the country east of the Jordan, carrying numerous caravans of goods. Travelers had to pay toll at certain strategic ports of entry, like Jericho at the crossing of the Jordan (Luke 19:1-2). During Solomon's reign Israel began to take her place among the great trading nations of the world, only to lose it again with the division of the kingdom, with the dispersion of the ten tribes to the north, and finally the captivity of the Jews, most of whom never returned to Palestine, but remained scattered throughout the East. Here they engaged in all kinds of occupations including business pursuits.

At the time of St. Paul the people of Palestine supplied the Phoenicians with their wheat and barley (Acts 12:20). She exported many other commodities in great quantities, such as olive oil, wine, and honey, wool and linen, asphalt from the Dead Sea region, dates from Jericho. Some of her imports were precious stones and ivory from the East, incense and spices, costly cloth and fine garments from Babylon (Is. 60:6).

Local Business — Haggling over Prices. — While the export and import trade rose and fell in importance according to world conditions, everybody at home did some buying, and many people devoted themselves to selling to the home

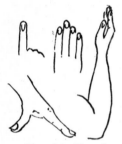

Fingerbreadth, palm, span, and cubit

market. Accustomed as we are to going into a retail food, clothing, or hardware store and finding the prices of everything clearly marked, doing our buying if we want the article or walking out of the store if we do not, we can scarcely appreciate the perfect planning and finesse which has always accompanied even the smallest business deal in the Near East. Haggling over prices was a ritual without which no bargain was satisfactory or complete, either to the buyer or to the seller.

Lineal Measurement. — The ancient Near East never knew an absolute and lasting standard of measurement, weight, or coinage, hence all information given in the following paragraphs is approximate only.

Since lineal measure was based on parts of the human body, it was varied according to time and country. The smallest unit was the fingerbreadth, somewhat less than an inch (Jer. 52:21). Four of these fingerbreadths made up a handbreadth, or palm (Ex. 37:12). Three palms made one span, the distance spanned by the outstretched hand from the tip of the thumb to the tip of the index finger (Ex. 28:16). Two of these spans totaled a cubit, which was the distance between the elbow and the tip of the longest finger. Many different cubits were used in the Near East, varying from 18 inches slightly upwards. The Egyptian royal cubit measured 20.7 inches. Six cubits made one reed (Ezek. 41:8), roughly the equivalent of our convenient ten-foot pole.

Larger distances were figured in the terms of a man's step or pace, approximately 30 inches (2 Sam. 6:13). "A little way" seems to have been somewhat over three miles (Gen. 48:7), about the distance one could conveniently walk in an hour. The "day's journey" was the distance which one could cover in approximately the seven or eight hours during which people traveled, counting the morning and afternoon, with a very long noon rest deducted. Thus the distance covered in a day might be about 20 miles. A Sabbath day's journey seems to have been approximately two thirds of a mile. (Acts 1:12).

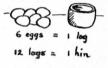

6 eggs = 1 log

12 logs = 1 hin

Liquid measure

Liquid and Dry Measure. — The smallest common unit for measuring liquids was the log. The Jews figured the log as the amount of water displaced by six hen's eggs, roughly the equivalent of our pint. Twelve logs made one hin, approximately six quarts, or one and one-half gallons. Six hins made one bath, about nine gallons. The "firkins," mentioned in the story of the wedding of Cana (John 2:6), were approximately the same measure as a bath, roughly 10 gallons. The largest measure was the homer or cor, the equivalent of ten baths, or about 90 gallons.

Units of dry measure were the following: The cab was somewhat under two quarts. Six cabs made one seah, not quite 10 quarts. Three seahs made one ephah, roughly the equivalent of a bushel. Ten ephahs made one homer, the largest common unit, about 10 bushels. The Roman *modius,* translated "bushel," in Matt. 5:15, is really about a peck, one quarter of our bushel, a size very handy around the home.

It is perhaps best not to burden our minds by attempting

to remember all of these units of measurement, since it is easy to find their exact equivalents in any Bible dictionary.

Money. — The coinage of the ancient world is an interesting and complicated study. The size and varied shapes of the coins, their supposed weight in silver or gold or copper, the proportions of these precious metals to the baser metals alloyed with them, all vary with the time and place of their manufacture, the integrity of the one responsible for their coinage, and the length of time they have been in use. Ancient coins did not have milled edges, and there was no way of knowing how much metal might have been worn or even filed off. Values can therefore be only approximate, especially since the buying power of a coin also varied from time to time, through periods of inflation and depression. It is difficult to express modern equivalents except in terms of a laborer's wage, "a penny a day," as we have it in the Parable of the Laborers in the Vineyard (Matt. 20:2).

In earliest times lumps of silver served as money. These had to be weighed each time they were used, since small chunks could easily be chipped off. But as early as when Abraham bought the Cave of Machpelah as a family burial place at the time of Sarah's death, he paid for it in "shekels current with the merchant" (Gen. 23:16), that is, in silver pieces weighing a shekel and so marked. A shekel of silver seems to have had a value of about sixty-five cents. The bekah was a half shekel, or about thirty-three cents. The gerah was one twentieth of a shekel, or about three and a fourth cents.

In Old Testament times the talent, or "round thing," seems to have been a metal ring weighing 3,000 shekels. Thus a talent of silver would be worth $2,000. Gold, in ancient as well as in modern times, worth about fifteen times as much as silver, had its shekel valued at about $10 and its talent at about $30,000. With buying power many times as great as in our own day, a talent of silver represented wealth, while a talent of gold meant fabulous riches.

In the New Testament the smallest copper coin was the Greek lepton, supposed to have been worth about one eighth of a cent. The widow put two of these "mites" into the treasury (Mark 12:42; Luke 12:6), a total contribution of one "farthing," or quadrans, a copper coin valued at about one quarter of a cent. The denarius, a common Roman silver coin, misleadingly translated "penny" in Matt. 20:2, was worth about 16 or 17 cents, about the equivalent of the Greek drachma. The silver stater, which Peter found in the mouth of the fish (Matt. 17:27), was worth four drachmas, or about 65 cents, the same as the shekel of silver.

During the centuries just before the birth of Christ, and in New Testament times, money from the Greek and Roman world, as well as that from the East, flowed freely in the markets of Palestine. The uncertain and changing values of the various coins provided plenty of opportunity for the shrewed money-changers in the Temple, the grafting publicans, and the money-wise merchants to become wealthy at the expense of the ignorant and the unfortunate.

REVIEW QUESTIONS AND EXERCISES

1. Explain why the Jews of Bible times did not develop a great group of sculptors and painters. How does this fact influence our knowledge of the appearance of great heroes of faith?
2. Describe the process of making
    a) parchment
    b) papyrus paper
   What kind of instruments were used in writing? In what form did the Jews make up their writings?
3. Be able to describe two of each of the following:
    a) wind instruments
    b) stringed instruments
    c) percussion instruments
4. Give an account of the use of singing and dancing in Bible times as a mode of emotional expression.
5. Who among the New Testament writers was a physician? How do wo know this?
6. With what kinds of timing devices were the Jews acquainted? On what did they base their
    a) day
    b) month

7. Discuss a typical journey of Galilean villagers to one of the great feasts at Jerusalem, noting
   a) their method of traveling
   b) diversions along the way
   c) overnight stops
8. Which methods of travel on land and sea were used by Bible peoples?
9. Compare a typical Jewish business transaction with our method of doing business today.
10. Be able to give the approximate equivalents of the following units of lineal measurement:
    a) fingerbreadth
    b) handbreadth, or palm
    c) span
    d) cubit
    e) reed
    f) "a little way"
    g) "a day's journey"
    h) "a Sabbath day's journey"
11. Give a general description of the money used in Bible times. Why is it difficult for us to express ancient buying power in terms of modern denominations of currency?

PROBLEMS FOR FURTHER STUDY

1. Find a number of "nature" psalms, and group pertinent passages for a five-minute presentation to the teacher group.
2. In the Gospel according to St. Luke, study "the beloved physician's" interest in disease and suffering. Note especially his accurate descriptions of sickness, his interest in the ills of womanhood, and the space he devotes to such illnesses.
3. Read St. Luke's account of the storm and shipwreck in Acts 27—28. Compare St. Luke's incidental description of the ship, its personnel and its parts, with that found in Ezek. 27:5-9; 27:27; Is. 33:23, and Jonah 1:4-13.

CHAPTER VIII

Social Customs and Family Life

Each nation and each age in the history of mankind has its distinctive social customs, which may seem very strange to those who are unaccustomed to them. The Near East has varied far less in the accepted customs from century to century than we Westerners would think possible. Rural and village life in Palestine today still reflects many of the habits and practices familiar to us from our acquaintance with Old Testament or New Testament Bible history.

CARE OF THE BODY: DRESS AND ADORNMENT

Washing, Bathing, and Anointing. — People of all times
" countries have found it necessary to wash and
ᵈegree of regularity. This is true especially
ꞋꞋ Law of Moses commanded bathing
ⁿliness, but as a religious ceremony
symbolized purity from sin as
(Gen. 35: 2). On special occa-
ʳy special purifications were
Ɪͅgan Pilate washed his hands
ḟ his own innocence of the
24), just as David spoke of
ʼence (Ps. 73: 13). Bathing
ʼor the purpose of ordinary
Levitical purity. Well-
ꞮꞮight have bathing facilities
or in special rooms of the
In the remains of the old
Ɪ̇ime of the Exodus, a stone
ꞮꞮꞮꞮꞮꞮ ꞮꞮꞮꞮꞮꞮ ꞮꞮꞮꞮꞮꞮ, wꞮꞮꞮ arrangements for running water
and drains for waste. The Greeks and Romans at the time
of Jesus had extensive and luxurious public baths, which to
some extent were copied in the Romanized larger cities of
Palestine. Poorer people of the villages depended upon
natural streams or bodies of water or upon sponge bathing
in the home.

After the bath the body was anointed with perfumed oil
(Ruth 3: 3). Some perfumes were produced in Palestine,
though many were imported from Sheba (1 Kings 10: 10).
The most costly of all was nard, the "spikenard," with which
Mary of Bethany anointed Jesus, which was so strongly
scented that "the house was filled with the odor of the ointment" (John 12: 3). The poor used ordinary olive oil instead
of the perfumed variety. The head, too, received its anointing
with oil, perfumed or otherwise, especially on festival days
or as a sign of special favor (Ps. 23: 5; Eccl. 9: 8). While
Absalom's long hair was greatly admired (2 Sam. 14: 26),

Elisha's baldness became the subject for the cruel funmaking of the young people of the city (2 Kings 2:23). The Jews ordinarily cut their hair rather short with a razor (Ezek. 44:20), but they did not shave their heads bare, as the Egyptians did. The women always wore their hair long. Thus Mary of Bethany was able to wipe Jesus' feet with her hair after she had anointed them with the precious ointment (John 12:1-3; John 11:2). In the early Church short hair was recognized as a sign of doubtful morals, while "if a woman have long hair, it is a glory for her, for her hair is given her for a covering" (1 Cor. 11:15). Women usually

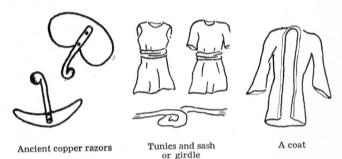

Ancient copper razors   Tunics and sash   A coat
                             or girdle

braided their hair or put it up in some form of a knot or "tire," as Jezebel did (2 Kings 9:30).

Clothing of Men. — The dress of men in Bible times was very simple. Men wore no underwear or trousers of any kind. The tunic was a long close-fitting woven shirt reaching to the knees. It had either short sleeves or no sleeves at all. The girdle was a sash, made of linen, like that of Jeremiah (Jer. 13:1), or a belt of leather, like that worn by John the Baptist (Matt. 3:4). The next garment, the coat, appears to have been cut to fit loosely, like a modern dressing gown or bathrobe. A second sash held it in place, either completely closed or partly open in front. The fold above the sash served as a pocket in which to carry food, a lamb, or even a measure of grain (Luke 6:38). The whole coat might be used to carry grain or other burdens by tying it together at the sleeves and corners and carrying it on the back, as is still done in the East (Ex. 12:34; Judg. 8:25). For dress wear the coat was made with long loosely flowing sleeves and was held together at the front by a very broad outer sash of contrasting material. Blue fringes adorned the borders of the garment to remind the Israelites to do all of God's commandments (Num. 15:38-39). Rich men wore finer fabrics, more expensively tailored, and sometimes richly embroidered in colored silk and gold. They maintained a large wardrobe of expensive clothes for their own use or to give away to friends or guests. The cloak was originally probably

Leather sandals   Fiber sandals

a sheepskin or blanket. It was of special importance to the poor and, if taken as security for a debt, could not be kept overnight; for without it, "wherein shall he sleep?" (Ex. 22:25-27.)

The more well-to-do wore sandals consisting of a leather sole fastened to the foot with thongs of the same material. Sandals were also woven of various fibers. In times of sorrow even King David went barefoot (2 Sam. 15:30), as the poor often did from necessity.

The headdress might be of any one of a number of types, depending on the time and place in which it was worn. The turban consisted of a long towellike strip of woolen material wound about the head. This is in very common use in the Near East today, but we are not sure how prevalent it was in Bible times. Another headdress was a square of cloth, folded into a triangle and held over the head by a "halo" of woven goat hair so that one triangle fell down the back and one at either side of the face, while a visorlike projection protected the eyes against the glare of the sun.

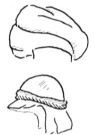

Clothing of Women. — The dress of women was very similar in design to that of the men. The material was of finer weave, and the dresses were worn longer, reaching to the ankles. The girdle was much wider, made of finer material, and consisted of more folds than that of the men. The long coat, or outer dress, was made of very finely woven wool, fine linen, or silk, often of scarlet, embroidered in gold and costly needlework (Ps. 45:13-14; 2 Sam. 1:24; Ezek. 16:13).

Turban, and linen headdress held by a woven band of goat's hair

The sandals of wealthy women were like those of the men but of the finest badger skin (Ezek. 16:10). Isaiah warned the worldly overdressed women of his day that the Lord would take away all of their luxurious clothing and ornament. He mentions twenty-one such items, including "changeable suits of apparel, mantles, wimples or shawls, fine linen underclothing, and hoods and veils" (Is. 3:18-24).

About the house or at work on the farm or in the vineyard the women dressed like the men, with no veils, and probably no headdress of any kind except as a protection against the extreme heat.

Ornament and Jewelry. — Besides finely embroidered clothing, men of high station commonly wore two additional ornaments, the seal and the staff. The seal, or signet (Gen. 38:18), was worn in a ring on the right hand (Jer. 22:24; Esther 3:10). It was used to sign letters and documents (1 Kings 21:8), as well as to seal bags of merchandise (Job 14:17). The staff, originally a weapon of defense, was carried as an ornament like the walking

Seal and staff

cane of two generations ago, (Gen. 38:18). The Babylonians, and probably the wealthy Israelites as well, had finely carved and engraved staffs, the head of which might be capped with gold or other precious metals. Men in neighboring nations, particularly the desert tribesmen, wore earrings, necklaces, and heavy gold chains, but, as far as we know, this was not done generally among the Israelites.

The ornaments of women were much more numerous and elaborate than those of men. Israelite women wore earrings of gold set with precious stones or inlaid with ivory (Ezek. 16:12), or ending

Ancient jewelry

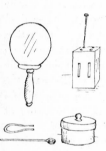

in long pendants or medallions (Is. 3:19). Nose rings were inserted through one nostril only or through the septum between the nostrils (Is. 3:21; Ezek. 16:12). Women also wore elaborate necklaces of precious metal or strings of pearls and other jewels (Ezek. 16:11; Song of Sol. 1:10) and bracelets and anklets of gold, finely engraved or set with precious stones (Is. 3:18-19).

Mirror, kohl bottle,
tweezers, ointment box

Extremes in the Use of Cosmetics and Adornment. — As in every age, some women of Israel overdid their ornamentation and make-up. They copied the customs of Egypt and of Babylonia, just as American women have copied those of Paris. They paid exorbitant prices for oils and creams from far countries. They painted their eyebrows and eyelashes and used dark-blue eyeshadow, or *kohl*, to an extent which was highly artificial. A mirror of polished brass was used (Ex. 38:8). Artificiality went over into everyday life in all of its aspects so that the society

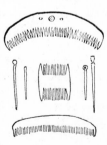

Ancient combs
and hairpins

women of Israel, "walking with stretched-forth necks and wanton eyes, walking and mincing as they go, and making a tinkling with their feet" (Is. 3:16), deserved the severe censure which was given to them by the Prophets Isaiah and Ezekiel. (Read Is. 3:16-26; Ezek. 16:15-23.) Living for dress and adornment, the sophisticate had made herself useless to society and had thrown herself open to all the temptations that beset those who love themselves above others and even above their God.

BETROTHAL AND MARRIAGE

The Marriageable Age. — In Bible times there were no caste restrictions on marriage between classes among the Israelites, although, naturally, people of one station tended to marry within the group of those in approximately the same circumstances. Marriage took place much earlier than is the custom among Western peoples. There is no indication in the Mosaic Law as to the minimum age when marriage might be contracted, but the *Talmud* states that the bride should be at least twelve years and one day old, and the bridegroom thirteen years and one day. It was considered a disgrace, or at least a serious disregard of custom and of duty, for a man not to be married by the age of twenty. In general, young people seem to have been married about the time they attained their full physical growth; girls by the age of fifteen or sixteen and men a year or two older.

The Contract, or Betrothal, as Binding as Marriage. — Among the Jews the parents always showed an active interest in the marriage of their children, the arrangement of which was considered one of their main responsibilities. The marriage agreement was made between the parents of the bride and groom, rather than by the young people themselves with the consent of their parents. Thus Abraham arranged for the marriage of his forty-year-old son Isaac (Gen. 24:2 ff.). Hagar secured a marriage for her son Ishmael (Gen. 21:21); and Isaac issued a command to Jacob as to whom he should or should not marry (Gen. 28:1).

It seems, though, that the young bride-to-be even at the time of the Patriarchs customarily gave her consent to the marriage, as Rebekah did (Gen. 24:57-58). As a token of his engagement the young man gave his betrothed a present, and he might also give one to the parents (Gen. 34:11-12).

When a betrothal had been properly arranged, it was just as binding as marriage, and any breach of morality by the bride was considered as adultery punishable by death (Deut. 22:23 f.). Marriage involved a lifelong obligation for both parties. God's arrangement that "a man leave his father and his mother and shall cleave unto his wife and they shall be one flesh" (Gen. 2:24) was rigidly observed by godly people of Bible times. No one has a right to separate man and wife (Matt. 19:6), and though the Law of Moses recognized the possibility of divorce, Jesus says it was because of the people's hardheartedness (Matt. 19:8; Mark 10:5-7) and permissible only on account of fornication (Matt. 5:31-32).

The Wedding Ceremony; Friends of the Bridegroom and Other Attendants. — At the prearranged hour the bridegroom came to the house of the bride, dressed in his wedding garments and escorted by his friends (Matt. 9:15). The girl friends of the bride, as in the Parable of the Wise and Foolish Virgins (Matt. 25:1 ff.), went out to meet him, also dressed in festive clothing, wearing veils and carrying lamps or torches with which to light up his way. At the door the bride in her wedding dress and veil greeted him, and her whole group, as well as his, went "with the voice of mirth and the voice of gladness, the voice of the bridegroom and the voice of the bride," to his home (Jer. 7:34). In early times marriage festivals seem to have lasted quite a long time, seven days in the case of Samson (Judg. 14:12). We have in Holy Scripture no accurate description of the wedding ceremony itself except that the bride's father or responsible relative gave her away with his parental blessing (Gen. 24:59-60).

The Marriage Feast. — Great numbers of people took part in the marriage supper, "all the men of the place" in the case of Jacob's marriage (Gen. 29:22). They were seated according to their rank or according to the honor which the groom wished to bestow upon them (Luke 14:7-9). In the company were the relatives, neighbors, and any visitors who might be with the family at the time. The meals were as elaborate as the family could afford, and it was considered a disgrace not to have enough for all. Thus at the marriage of Cana we find Mary very much concerned when the wine supply began to fail, because, as a friend of the family, she felt partly responsible for this unheard-of emergency (John 2:3-5).

CHILDREN

The Curse of Childlessness and the Blessing of Children. Among God's people of all ages it has been recognized that "children are an heritage of the Lord" (Ps. 127:3-5) and that it is the Lord who "maketh the barren woman to keep house and to be a joyful mother of children" (Ps. 113:9). To a Hebrew woman no curse could possibly be quite so great as that of having no children, as we can see in the cases of Sarah (Gen. 16:2); Rachel (Gen. 30:1); and Hannah (1 Sam. 1:6). Such women felt that they were "a reproach among men," as Elisabeth puts it (Luke 1:25). The joy and gratitude of these women, who knew that in answer to their prayers this great curse had been removed, shows us how bitterly they had suffered (Gen. 21:6; Gen. 30:23; 1 Sam. 1:24-28). Besides the desire for offspring, which is common among all races, the Jewish woman had an added reason, for she felt that she might be the ancestress of the promised Savior or perhaps even His own mother. It was natural therefore that a large family was considered to be a very special blessing of God and a special token of His grace and mercy (Prov. 17:6; Eccl. 6:3).

Care and Nursing of the Baby. — From the very earliest times midwives assisted Hebrew mothers at the birth of their children, as they did in the case of Rachel (Gen. 35:17) and Tamar (Gen. 38:28). In Egypt at the time of the birth of Moses this profession, like other occupations, had been organized into a guild under their own leaders (Ex. 1:15). These people noticed that the Hebrew women bore their children with much less pain and delay than did women of other races (Ex. 1:19). This still appears to be true today.

Immediately after the birth the midwife bathed the child with warm water and rubbed it with salt and possibly with olive oil. She then wrapped it in swaddling clothes, consisting of long strips of cloth firmly wrapped about the child's body (Ezek. 16:2-5), just as Mary did at the birth of Jesus (Luke 2:7).

Hebrew mothers took great pride in caring for and nursing their own children, as did the aged Sarah (Gen. 21:7) and Hannah, the mother of Samuel (1 Sam. 1:2-3). Such a precious gift of God could not be left out of their sight.

On the eighth day of his life the boy underwent the rite of circumcision, according to God's command. Like our own children who have received Baptism, he now belonged to God's chosen people and was an heir of His gracious promises. At this time he also received his name. In early times it appears that the name was often given on account of some personal peculiarity (Esau, the red one, Gen. 25:25) or circumstance connected with the birth (Benjamin, Gen. 35:18) or with the experiences (Samuel, 1 Sam. 1:20) or with the hopes of the parents for the newborn child (Reuben, Gen. 29:32). At the birth of John the Baptist the relatives and friends took it for granted that the baby would be named after his father (Luke 1:59-63). This had no doubt become a common practice, just as it has among us today.

After a period of forty days in the case of a boy, and a period twice as long in the case of a girl baby, the mother went to the Temple and offered a sacrifice of purification according to the Levitical Law (Lev. 12:1-8). Mary, because of her poverty, offered "a sacrifice according to that which is said in the Law of the Lord, a pair of turtle doves or two young pigeons" (Luke 2:22-24; compare Lev. 12:8).

According to a custom which still exists among many primitive nations, the mother continued to nurse her child

as long as two or three years. Thus Hannah did not wean
little Samuel until she could entrust him to the aged Eli,
whom he was to serve at the Tabernacle at Shiloh (1 Sam.
1:23). The time of weaning was usually the occasion of
another special family gathering, similar to that provided by
Abraham at the weaning of Isaac (Gen. 21:8).

Early Training of Children. — Children, as special gifts
of God and the most precious possession of their parents,
enjoyed a happy home life. During the early years the
mother necessarily bore the responsibility not only for the
care of the household, but for the home training of the
children (Prov. 31). Pious mothers, like the mother of King
Solomon (Prov. 31:1) and the mother and the grandmother
of Timothy (2 Tim. 3:15), did what Christian mothers still do
as their greatest privilege: they brought their little children
to the Lord by teaching them His Word. At a very tender
age the children heard of the great things which God had
done for His people. Pious fathers, like Abraham, taught
their whole households, including the small children, to
"keep the way of the Lord, to do justice and judgment"
(Gen. 18:19). Children learned to look forward to the fulfillment of God's promises concerning the coming Redeemer.
Love and respect and obedience to their parents was their
highest earthly duty. When this attitude towards God, and
towards His earthly representatives, the parents, is learned
in early childhood, it can scarcely be forgotten; but when
it is not learned at an early age, it is very difficult for anyone
to understand it later.

While the mother influenced her sons less and less as
they grew older and began to work with their father, the
girls became her special responsibility. The girl received
training for one purpose, to become a wife and mother. The
very little girl had to learn to cook, which she did by helping
her mother. In her own home she observed, and took part
in, all the other household tasks, just as little girls under
normal circumstances still do today. She learned to sew,
knit, spin, weave, grind grain, prepare bread and other foods,

sweep and clean the house, and take care of the younger children, so that by the time she reached even the comparatively early marriageable age she was fully equipped to handle a household of her own.

Special Training of Boys. — While in later times, and especially under the influence of Hellenic customs, the boys of wealthy families were turned over to special teachers, among the earlier Israelites and perhaps among the poorer classes at all times the father took care of this duty himself. He taught his sons to read and write well enough to read the Law of God and to take their rightful place in the community. He carefully continued the religious instruction which he and his wife had begun in the boy's infancy. He also taught his sons how to make their living by a trade, even though he himself might earn his living by a profession. Thus Saul of Tarsus, of good family and trained in all the higher learning of the Jews and of the Greeks, was by trade a tentmaker and was not ashamed to support himself at various times during his ministry by working with his hands, along with his converts Aquila and Priscilla (Acts 18:3). Boys did not learn trades in a school, but in the shop at home or in the home of a friend or relative. The sons of farmers learned agriculture by doing it on the home farm. At a very early age shepherd boys became reliable and efficient enough to be left in complete charge of their father's flocks. Thus the Hebrew boy came to feel the dignity and privilege of work as well as the necessity of working to make a living. He became independent, self-reliant.

No attempt will be made in this book to discuss the synagog schools or other types of training institutions available to the people of Old Testament or New Testament times. The whole topic of public education, along with public religious worship in the Tabernacle and later in the Temple and community synagog, and of the higher education of teachers and priests will make up several chapters of a later course.

The Complete Education. — Ideally, the aim of education among the Hebrews was the fear of the Lord as the beginning of wisdom (Ps. 111:10; Prov. 1:7). With the fear and love of God as his motivation, the earnest believer learned to depart from evil (Job 28:28) and, in the measure in which he found grace, to lead a decent, upright life.

HOSPITALITY, RECREATION, AND PERIODIC FESTIVALS

Hospitality and Greetings. — Hospitality was characteristic of Bible peoples from the beginning, just as it still is in Bible lands today. Only a very boorish person would neglect to ask a traveler to stop for a meal or overnight, lest he might have to "lodge in the street" (Job 31:32). This traveler might be a stranger, yet the host invited him in, washed his feet, prepared a meal for him, took care of his donkey or other animal, and treated him like an honored member of the family until such a time as he could again send him on his journey. Such was the conduct of Abraham (Gen. 18:2 f.) and of Lot (Gen. 19:1 f.) when they "entertained angels unawares." Even Laban, crafty and dishonest as he was, showed the same hospitaltiy to his guest, Abraham's old servant (Gen. 24:31 f.). When once two Orientals have eaten together, there is a bond of friendship between them which dare not be broken. They are no longer strangers to each other, but there is "bread and salt between them."

When a Hebrew man approached another on the road, he bowed to the ground as a mark of his respect. He did not salute a stranger while riding upon his donkey, but first dismounted, just as the people of the East still do. The bowing seems to have been done by first kneeling, then falling with the face flat to the ground. People called down the blessings of God upon each other when they met in the street. Scripture records a number of such formal greetings. "God be gracious to thee" (Gen. 43:29); "Peace be with thee" (Judg. 19:20); "The Lord be with you" and "The Lord bless thee" (Ruth 2:4); and "Peace, peace be unto thee"

(1 Chron. 12:18). After the exchange of the blessing, the host asked numerous questions about the visitor's health, friends, and family. Occasionally, particularly if those who met were close relatives or friends, the salutation was much more intimate. Numerous cases are recorded where men kissed and embraced each other or, as the Scripture puts it, "fell upon each other's neck" (Gen. 33:4), just as people in the Near East and in southern Europe still do, a custom which seems strange to those of North European extraction. As a mark of respect towards their elders, young men stood up in their presence (Lev. 19:32). When finally it was time to say good-by, there was a repetition of the blessing and kissing and embracing, and often weeping, as in the case of St. Paul's departure from Ephesus (Acts 20:37).

Games and Toys of Children. — As we have seen in the previous section, the Hebrew parents taught their children the Law of God, respect for their parents and elders, how to do the work about the home and shop and, in general, how to take their places in a world of work and responsibility; but the

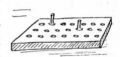

Child's ball and game board

child's day was not altogether taken up with these serious activities. Children played just as children play now. They had games and toys of all kinds. Game boards were somewhat similar to those used for our checkers and various marble games of today. The children played ball, though what the rules were we do not know. When a wedding procession with its joyful music and happy party passed by, the children played at "wedding"; and when a mournful funeral procession wound its way to the grave, the games of the children in the market place echoed its solemnity (Matt. 11:17; Luke 7:32). Girls played "house," as girls have done in all ages. Boys played at the trades of their fathers or of others whose activities they had observed. Thus boys and girls sang and chanted and piped and danced with the bound-

less energy characteristic of children the world over, and
grew up to take their places in organized society.

**Outdoor Mass Demonstrations, Games, Festivities of the
Harvest.** — On special occasions groups of people gathered
at the market places or about the gates of the city for conversation or for recreation (Acts 17:17; Matt. 20:3). At the
announcement of a victory, or upon the return of a victorious
army, the women went out to meet their returning husbands
and sons, singing and dancing to the accompaniment of cymbals
and tambourines all along the line of march (1 Sam. 18:6 f.).
When Solomon became king, the people "piped with pipes
and rejoiced with great joy, so that the earth rent with the
sound of them" (1 Kings 1:40). At the accession of the
Lord's avenger, King Jehu, "they hasted, and took every
man his garment and put it under him on the top of the
stairs, and blew with trumpets, saying, Jehu is King!"
(2 Kings 9:13.) Thus loyalty and devotion to the state as
well as national solidarity found expression. At the same
time the people were provided with a very necessary safety
valve for their pent-up emotions. Such enthusiasm was
sometimes short-lived, as when Jesus Himself entered Jerusalem in fulfillment of prophecy and "a very great multitude
spread their garments in the way, others cut down branches
from the trees and strewed them in the way, and the mul-
titudes that went before and that followed cried, saying,
Hosannah to the Son of David" (Matt. 21:8-9). No doubt
some of these same enthusiasts, fickle as they were, could
take part in the mob scene before Pilate with the terrible
cry "Crucify Him!" (Luke 23:21) and, in the frenzy of their
hatred, call down His blood upon themselves and upon their
children (Matt. 27:25).

The various festivals of the harvest provided opportunity and motivation for rejoicing and for group entertainment. The barley harvest came first, followed by the harvest
of wheat, of grapes, and of olives. Though the daytime was
spent in hard work, the evenings were enlivened by music,
singing, and sociability.

Formal Entertainment, Banquets. — Upon the occasion of a special banquet in celebration of a marriage, a weaning, or the visit of some influential person the host sent out elaborate invitations a week ahead of time so that nothing could possibly interfere with the attendance of the guests. When the great day came, the servant of the master repeated the invitation, "Come, for all things are now ready." It was rude to refuse an invitation at any time, inexcusable to do it at the last moment (the Great Supper, Luke 14:15-24). When the guests arrived, the host greeted them and commanded his servants to wash their feet. He then anointed their heads and conducted them personally to the banquet chamber.

Upon such a great occasion the food provided was not likely to be the usual stew, but "the fatted calf" (Luke 15:23) or a kid barbecued before the fire. No money and no pains were spared to make it enjoyable for all who attended. Places were carefully reserved for the honored guests, and "social climbers" enviously longed for higher sitting priority (Luke 14:7). At the feast those who attended engaged in light conversation. Riddles, stories, humor, and music enlivened the festival (Luke 15:23-25; Judg. 14:12-18).

Jesus' Lessons from the Banquet Feasts. — Since everyone was acquainted with the customs at banquets of the day, Jesus based a number of His teachings upon them. Thus He taught a powerful lesson on humility when He noted that the chief places were chosen by the Pharisees (Luke 14:7-14). From the story of the banquet given for the Prodigal Son, He taught the lesson of joy in the heavenly Father's heart at the return of the sinner and warned against the selfishness of the elder brother (Luke 15:11-32). He pictured the joys of heaven as a wedding festival, (Matt. 25:1-13). He warned against using the duties and pleasures of everyday life as excuses for putting off our coming to the Lord's great banquet feast (Luke 14:15-24). He taught the equality of all men by eating with "publicans and sinners" like Zacchaeus (Luke 19:1-10) and the mixed company at the

feast of Matthew (Mark 2:14-17) as well as with Pharisees
and the wealthy (Luke 7:36-50). He called attention to the
ruthless rejection of God's grace by the Jews in His Parable
of the Marriage of the King's Son (Matt. 22:1-14).

SICKNESS, DEATH, AND BURIAL; THE HOPE OF RESURRECTION

Causes of Sickness. — Just as sin is common to the whole
human family, so are its results, sickness and death. In
general, the climate of Palestine is more favorable than that
of other nations of the Near East. Except in the Jordan
Valley, with its tropical heat and humidity and malaria,
Palestine enjoys healthful and invigorating weather conditions, and the Bible people in general were a strong and
healthy race.

The inspired Prophet Moses threatened pestilence and
consumption and fever and inflammation, along with other
evils, as direct visitations of God to bring His people to
repentance (Deut. 28:21-22), and the whole nation (2 Sam.
24:15), or guilty individuals, such as Gehazi (2 Kings 5:27)
and Jehoahaz (2 Chron. 21:18-19), were sometimes punished
for gross and unrepented sin. Some of the common diseases
have received brief consideration in Chapter VII, Section
B, 2, Common Diseases. Any good Bible dictionary has a
more extended treatment.

Sympathy in Sickness and Mourning in Death. — When
anyone in the family took sick, the whole family group was
disturbed. So little was known about disease and its treatment that the approach of illness caused general fear and
even terror. A physician was called if available. Often,
however, one of the older members of the community who by
long experience knew most about diseases prescribed the
remedies. Nor did God's people neglect to use prayer in
the case of sickness, since they knew that God, who sent the
illness, could also cure it if it was His will (Ps. 103:3; Matt.
9:21). Contrary to our rigid sickroom regulations of today,
the whole family crowded into the room in order to show

their sympathy. At the bedside of the sick they wept and mourned, and comforted the afflicted one, while at the same time they unwittingly shut out fresh air and made his recovery more difficult.

When in spite of the prayers of the family and friends, and in spite of all the physician could do, the patient died, the mourning began immediately. The wailing set up in the house itself was taken up by the neighbors along the street until it penetrated throughout the whole community. The body was at once prepared for burial, which ordinarily took place on the day of death.

Burial Customs. — Though the Egyptians very carefully and thoroughly embalmed their dead and the custom was known among the Israelites, the latter never practiced it generally. They washed the dead, then dressed them or wrapped them in "grave clothes," as in the case of Lazarus (John 11:44). They then sprinkled the clothing or wrappings with sweet-smelling crystals of balm. The body was then laid on a bier or stretcher and carried by friends or relatives to the burial place (Luke 7:14). The mourn-

Rock-hewn grave

ers walked along beside the bier, weeping and wailing as they went. At the grave they reverently laid the body to rest. Beyond these facts we know very little about the details of the burial.

Various types of graves were used in Palestine. Abraham bought the cave of Macpelah as a burial place for his wife and family (Gen. 23:15-20). Caves continued to be used as burial places throughout Israelite history. Jesus compares the Pharisees to "whited sepulchers" (Matt. 23:27), referring to the clean, white-washed slab of limestone which covered the rock-hewn grave containing dead men's bones. Other holes were dug into the side of a rock, thus forming an artificial cave, in front of which a stone could be rolled to serve as a door. Such a stone closed and sealed the entrance to the family tomb of Joseph of Arimathaea, in which the disciples buried Jesus (Matt. 27:66; John 19:41-42). It was so heavy that the women who had come to finish the burial rites on Easter morning wondered who would roll it away for them (Mark 16:3). Some of the natural or artificial caves were very large, provided with shelves or niches on which the bodies could be laid and then individually sealed in by flat slabs of stone placed in front of them and plastered in around the edges.

The Hope of Resurrection. — For believers of Bible times, as well as for Christians today, the grave does not

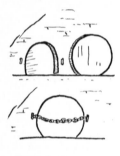

Grave door — open, closed, and sealed

end all. God's people do not sorrow "as others which have no hope" (1 Thess. 4:13), for they know that God, who created man and redeemed him, can and will also raise him up from the dead. This hope buoyed up the people in the Old Testament. The Patriarch Job voices the triumphant faith of the Christian in a passage which has given comfort to countless millions since — "I know that my Redeemer liveth and that He shall stand at the latter day upon the earth. And though, after my skin, worms destroy this body, yet in my flesh shall I see God, whom I shall see for myself, and mine eyes shall behold, and not another" (Job 19:25-27). David in his psalms gives the same assurance. Martha knows that Lazarus will rise again in the resurrection at the Last Day, though she does not realize that her brother is to become alive again so soon (John 11:24).

The prophets of old raised the dead through the power of God as a sign of the coming resurrection of all flesh. Jesus Himself raised the young man of Nain and Lazarus. He promised that He Himself would rise again, and He brought that promise to a glorious fulfillment on Easter morning.

Thus, in the Old and the New Testament alike, death has lost its sting, the grave has lost its victory, and the glorious Resurrection Day points the way to the everlasting home of the people of God.

REVIEW QUESTIONS AND EXERCISES

1. What facilities were available for bathing in Bible times? What is meant by "anointing" the body?

2. Describe the clothing of men —
   a) the tunic, or shirt
   b) the girdle
   c) the coat
   d) the cloak
   e) the headdress
   f) the sandals

   In which ways did the clothing of women differ from that of men?

3. Be able to give an account of
   a) the marriage contract, or betrothal
   b) the marriage ceremony
   c) the wedding feast in a well-to-do family

4. Describe the home education and training of the children by the father and the mother in Israel.

5. Describe the greetings, conversation, and farewells of men meeting by chance on the highway.

6. Give a general account of the toys and games of village boys and girls at the time of Jesus.

7. Describe the preparations and the menu at a typical banquet in New Testament times. Pick out three lessons which Jesus taught in connection with such feasts.

8. Contrast a sickroom in Judea at the time of Jesus with one in our own homes today.

9. Be able to give some details as to burial customs —
   a) preparation for burial
   b) funeral procession
   c) various types of graves

10. Quote at least one Scripture passage which shows that the Old Testament people believed in a future life and in the resurrection of the body.

PROBLEMS FOR FURTHER STUDY

1. Compare the extremes in women's clothing, ornament, and general sophistication current in late Old Testament times with the same signs in our civilization today. Which principles should guide a Christian woman in her choice of clothing, jewelry, and cosmetics? Discuss how you can foster incidentally an awareness of these principles among the teen-age girls.

2. With the help of a Bible dictionary and concordance, make a study of leprosy in connection with the cases reported in both the Old and New Testaments. Note the Jewish laws regarding the diagnosis and isolation of the disease.

3. Look up and study all the Scripture accounts of the raising of the dead. What is the difference between Jesus' acts of resurrection and those of other men?